New
Beginnings

New Beginnings

JOSEPH P. BISHOP

Published by
√chosen books
Lincoln, Virginia 22078
Distributed by Word Books • Waco, Texas 76703

Scripture quotations are from the King James or The Revised Standard Version of the Bible. Scripture quotations from the RSV, copyrighted 1946, 1952, © 1971, 1973, are used by permission of the Division of Christian Education of the National Council of the Churches of Christ in the U.S.A.

Library of Congress Cataloging in Publication Data

Bishop, Joseph P
  New beginnings.

    1.   Christian life—1960–   2.   Conversion.
3.   Bishop, Joseph P.   I.   Title.
BV4501.2.B533   248′.24   79–23104

ISBN 0–912376–49–X

To Peggy

*who made new beginnings
possible for me*

Contents

Acknowledgments

MY GREATEST DEBT in writing this book is to my editor, Elizabeth Sherrill. Her kind, consistent, sensitive spirit, combined with her awesome skills as an editor, have made her an invaluable teacher and friend to me. She understood so readily and profoundly what I was trying to say; she helped me to say it better. Nor did she ever try to suggest something which was contrary to my natural style and message. Her respect for my own depths enabled me to do what I could never have done had I not felt the background of her Christian commitment and talents. No writer about Christian experience was ever more blessed than I have been by Elizabeth Sherrill.

Nor can I fail to express my undying appreciation to my dear friends, Hans and Lisi Suter, whose gracious hospitality to me on repeated visits to Switzerland has given me the space I needed for inspiration, solitude, beauty and quiet in the labor of writing. But more than space, they have given me love which surrounded my days of creation in their midst with an aura of devotion which I return with a whole heart.

I wish also to acknowledge the debt I owe to those persons whose stories of struggle and rebirth I have told in this book. Their kindness in permitting me to write in depth about their experiences has made this little book possible. In most cases they have asked me to use pseudonyms, but to those who knew them, their real names are easily recognizable. For the privilege of sharing their lives I extend to them a rose of thankfulness.

Finally, my deep gratitude to Milly Cordtz, my typist and friend. She spent many long evenings and weekends in her home typing and retyping these pages. Her joy and encouragement to me in this long labor have been priceless.

New Beginnings

As I WRITE THESE words I find myself in a house in Switzerland above Lago Maggiore with the Italian Alps in the distance. It is early April. The fruit on the lemon trees is small, tight and green; the lake below my feet motionless as death, waiting for the resurrection of May.

It is the same cherished place in which I wrote my last book six years ago. When I tried to catch the meaning of my experience sitting above these shores in 1973, it was death which preoccupied me. The sudden and accidental end of my son Peter's life in his 18th year and the loss of my wife Carola after a long and torturous battle with cancer posed many problems for my emotional and spiritual life. In my solitude and sleeplessness during those nights and days I learned that the only way out of my turmoil was the way through the center. If I tried to side-step the pain I only became more enmeshed in my misery. The enduring mountains kept telling me, "Face the truth of it all, do not shrink from the realities you must confront in yourself."

The truth of that experience grows deeper with me every year; for it is in this deep core of our being that we make an astonishing discovery: We are not alone. Someone Else is with us, opening new doors of guidance we could not have predicted. Giving release from guilt we could never have believed possible. Replacing doubt by a victory of faith we could never have obtained alone. Making possible new beginnings we thought could never happen.

New beginnings! This is the hope we are offered—that out of crisis and pain can come newness. New joy in place of sorrow, new life to follow death.

I know it is no easy task to see God in the shadows as well as in the sunshine. When those three horsemen—defeat, disease, and death—overtake us, we cannot escape the feeling that the Almighty has deserted us. Instead of help we start to anticipate a repetition of our defeats and desertions. We begin to look for the worst instead of the best in situations and people—with disastrous results. The enemy we fear becomes our focal point until presently we draw to ourselves the very things we hate. The manipulativeness we loathe in another person becomes characteristic of the way we gain our own ends. We spend more energy fearing betrayal than we do trusting the best within ourselves and others. Years of bitter experience teach us to be cynics, and we are tempted to concede that everyone must be first, foremost, and always for himself because there is no one else who is for us.

Isn't all this the result of our incapacity to see the whole realm of our experience permeated by the living God, leavening, lifting, transforming every aspect of our lives? Do we not know that nothing is excluded, not even our hatreds and hostilities? Nothing can happen to us, positively or negatively, in joy or in sorrow, which is exterior to God.

At all times and in all places God is at work in our lives helping us to find new beginnings. If the mysterious drama of the Christ-life means anything, it is that God's will for new beginnings is the strongest, most consistent power mankind has ever known.

And yet the majority of humankind—including, alas, a large proportion of sincere, seeking churchgoers—go through their entire lives unaware of this most profound and ultimate truth. The sins of the world, our own sins, the whole litany of selfishness, pride, the misuse of power and the oppression of the defenseless—from the labor camps in Siberia to the genocide practiced in our own country against the Indian—all tempt us to doubt God's presence in our midst. If this be the real world in which we all live, how can God be any part of it?

But the core of the Christian message is that He *is* present in our world; and not only present, but continually, irrevocably on our side, offering us new beginnings in place of old defeats. St. Paul knew the catalogue of human woe all too well. His lists of sin are embarrassingly reminiscent of our own experience, yet he could declare the invincible love of Christ for our fallen race. After saying in the seventh chapter of Romans, ". . . the good that I would I do not: but the evil which I would not, that I do," he nevertheless lifts the trumpet of trust to his lips in the eighth chapter and says, "Who shall separate us from the love of Christ? Shall tribulation, or distress, or persecution, or famine, or nakedness, or peril, or sword? . . . Nay, in all these things we are more than conquerors through Him that loved us . . . If God be for us, who can be against us?"

If God be for us. . .

My intent in writing this book is to add my witness to the voices down through the ages which have affirmed that this impossible supposition is a simple statement of reality. It will be a very personal record; you can't share a truth with others which you haven't learned yourself.

As I look down upon this cherished lake in its frame of snow-clad mountains, I have come full circle. One chapter in my life has closed; death turned the page. A new chapter has opened; love turned the page. A new marriage has come to me and new beginnings are all around me. At no time is the hand of God's caring so palpable as at these great turning points in life. I want to write about my own most intimate experiences of endings and beginnings and, with their permission, those of the men and women with whom my life has been linked in almost 40 years as counselor to people in crisis. It is crisis that wrenches from us the cry, "Where is God? Does He care about me?" I want to set down an answer written in the lives of people I know best.

Chapter 1

Forgiveness:
The Woman Who Was Dirt

NANCY AND KENNETH seemed particularly well suited to one another when they asked me to perform their wedding. They had much in common: similar religious and economic backgrounds, similar educational experiences. They had known each other since their first year in college and wanted the same things out of life. They both liked skiing, golfing, tennis, sailing. They were neither of them intellectually inclined; I doubt if either read a book after college. The only difference I could detect on casual observation was that Kenneth's father had come up the economic ladder the hard way, on his own, while Nancy's father, the son of a well-to-do manufacturer, had begun with a considerable head start.

One day, about five years after the marriage, I received a phone call from Kenneth. They had settled in an apartment not far from the church I pastor in Rye, New York, and where they occasionally attended services. I had baptized their only child, a daughter. Ken, however, was calling not from home but from his office in nearby New York City.

"Joe, I've got to see you! I can't concentrate on work. It's stupid for me to stay here at the office. I'll come anytime you say." I could tell his voice was close to breaking.

"Come out on the next train, Ken," I said.

When he came in, he didn't say a word in answer to my welcome. He sat down, leaned his head against the back of the overstuffed wing chair in my study, and closed his eyes. "It's so messy I hardly know where to begin . . ."

Ken is a small-boned man, wiry and nimble, with close-cropped, curly hair and light blue eyes. The only unusual quality about his appearance is a noticeably high forehead. He took a big breath and plunged ahead. "I suppose I might as well begin with the worst. Nancy has become an alcoholic, and she's sleeping around."

"How long has this been going on?"

"The drinking or the sex routine?"

"Both."

"Well, she started becoming a really heavy drinker about three years ago. I didn't notice anything at first; but after Sally was born she was depressed all the time. The responsibility of the kid seemed more than she could take. She began having two drinks before dinner in the evening and about three after dinner before going to bed. Never bothered to use a jigger, just filled the glass about half full for each drink."

"Why haven't you come to me before, or to anyone else, Ken?"

"What was the use of my going to someone? Nancy's the one who's got the problem."

This was said with anger and heat. I leaned over toward Ken and gently said, "I'm aware of that, Ken, and your pain gets to me. I couldn't be more sorry. Let me put my question this way: What have you done to try to get help for Nancy?"

Ken shifted his position in the chair and launched forth again. "I've tried everything in the last year I knew to try, Joe. I told her to see a psychiatrist, and when she refused to do that, I asked her if she would come to see you. But she said she didn't want you to know about it because your respect is too important to her. I told her I would call a friend of ours who's in AA, but she only got furious and told me she was no alcoholic."

All this was said at breakneck speed. Ken came up for air, but instead of taking a big breath, he unexpectedly broke down in tears.

He reached for tissues which are always on the table by the chair. Finally, when he had composed himself, he said, "But that's not the worst. You see, for over a year now she's been a pushover for any man who wants her."

"How do you know that, Ken?"

"Different men call the house. She comes home at 3 A.M. with no explanation. Then last night I saw her car at Birnie Lambert's house at 1:30 A.M. when I got in a day early from a business trip to Minneapolis. You know he's divorced and lives alone. Something just exploded in my head. I went crashing up to Birnie's door making an unbelievable racket, hammering on the door and shouting to Birnie to let me in. When there was no answer I took a rock and threw it through the living room window."

Ken stopped. "Do you mind if I have a cigarette?" His hands were shaking as he lit it.

"Lights went on upstairs, and in a minute Birnie stood in the doorway with just his pants on. I said I knew Nancy was there and she'd damn well better get herself downstairs and go home with me or somebody was going to get murdered around there." The rage in Ken was still burning.

"Anyhow, to make a long story short, Nancy came down pronto after that, and when we got home I beat her up. I didn't break any bones, but that wasn't because I didn't intend to."

There was a long, tight pause. I broke it by asking, "What's become of little Sally through all this?"

"I'm sorry, I thought you knew. Nancy's mother has had Sally for over a year now."

We continued talking, then and at subsequent meetings, searching for a clue as to where and how things had started toward such an avalanche of disaster. It had seemed so right to all of us at the beginning. What had happened?

As soon as possible I went to see Nancy. She was expecting me and, childlike, fell weeping into my arms. I hadn't seen her in some time. Her complexion bore the overheated color of the alcoholic. Her hands shook when she handed me a cup of coffee. She was excessively thin, her once lustrous brown hair lifeless. This formerly articulate, intelligent girl now had difficulty focusing on any subject for long. The apartment was a scene of squalor and depression.

About an hour after I arrived I said with unconcealed anxiety, "Nancy, dear Nancy, what are we going to do?"

"I wish I knew," she replied.

"You must have some ideas," I insisted.

"What does it matter? I know I'm rotten. I don't deserve anyone's love. I just wish everybody would go away and let me alone."

"Nancy, there's no point in talking about anything else until we begin to do something about the drinking. Are you ready to admit you need some help with that?"

Nancy stared at the floor. Then she said, "I can't imagine what life would be like without liquor."

"But, Nancy, do you *want* to find out what it would be like?"

There was no answer. Further conversation proved useless, and I left soon afterwards.

There were many more visits after that. I soon learned to telephone beforehand. If her speech was incoherent I knew there was no point in going. Sometimes she was effusive, telling me how grateful she was for my interest, how much she loved me. At other times she was abusive, telling me in unrepeatable language that I should get out of her life and leave her alone. She lived by herself now; Ken had moved to an apartment he shared with a bachelor friend.

One night the phone rang about 2 A.M. It was nothing unusual; I was sure it was Nancy. These late phone calls were always the same: pleading for love, for reassurance.

But this time the call was from the police. "We have a woman here named Nancy ———, and she says you'll come for her, Reverend Bishop. She's in pretty bad shape."

A few minutes later I walked into the police station. Nancy was sitting on a bench opposite the sergeant's desk. The side of her head was bruised and she was holding her left arm as though it were injured.

"What happened?" I asked the sergeant.

"She didn't make the corner coming around on the Old Post Road and slammed her car into the wall."

A straightforward statement of the facts, but under his words I picked up his disgust and rage. This wasn't the first time the police had dealt with Nancy. She was released under my care without bail and charged with driving while under the influence of alcohol.

I almost had to carry Nancy from my car to her door. She kept blubbering, "I'm sorry, Joe, I'm sorry."

Her driver's license was revoked; her inoperative car was parked at the side of a repair shop. Ken paid her rent but wouldn't give her any money. So she began to beg and borrow from anyone and everyone who would give her cash. I never gave her money, but many times I brought groceries to her kitchen. It baffled me how she stayed alive. Often the food I brought was untouched a week later.

She soon reached the bottom of everyone's good will. No one would give her any more money and still she drank. "Where does she get the money to buy it?" I asked myself many times.

I spoke of my puzzlement to Ken who informed me, "Simple. She goes to bars, picks up any man who'll buy her drinks, and they wind up in the apartment."

It was like a knife through my heart. Not a week had gone by without some effort on my part to reach Nancy. I had pled with her, begged her to let me hospitalize her, told her how deeply I believed in the Nancy I once knew.

The discovery of her "night life" added new fuel to my determination. The following day I arrived at her apartment about 10:30 A.M. I had learned that the only time to catch Nancy in a moment of lucidity was when she had her usual pot of morning coffee. All the way to her door I prayed, "Lord Jesus, Nancy needs a very special new beginning; may it be now. May she be ready to accept you today." It didn't matter that I had prayed that prayer hundreds of times before. Something in me said with new urgency, "Maybe this is the time."

Nancy's eyes lit up when she saw me. It was the right hour of the day; she was fairly sober. "I had a dream about you last night, Joe. You were in church, standing behind the altar, and you were lifting up the communion cup and looking right at me. I wanted to run, but I couldn't, and I woke up screaming."

My pulse quickened. I felt this was the channel God had opened.

"What do you think the dream meant, Nancy?"

"I don't know," she parried. "What do you think it means?"

"I think it means that there is a wistful, deep-down longing in you, a voice saying—'I wish, I wish, I wish.' A longing to long, a yearning to yearn. Something under all the guilt and all the self-hatred wants to come home."

Nancy broke down at that. I tried to lead the conversation back to the dream, but in a few minutes I knew she had turned me off and I left.

I'll never know why, but I knew that morning was a turning point. The dream was a sign. I thanked God for it and decided to drop in to see Nancy about that time of day two or three times a week. Our steps would have to be measured in inches, but I knew we were on the way.

The next week Nancy had on a sweater I had never seen before. "No, it's not new," she said. "It's been lying in my bureau drawer a couple of years. I just never wore it until today." She glanced up at me. "Do you like the color? Ken gave it to me."

"Looks great to me." And I thought to myself, *This is another sign.*

"Nancy, could you possibly try to believe with me that a whole new beginning is possible for you?" I began. "God is always trying to provide us with fresh beginnings if we honestly want to find them."

"But, Joe, how can I begin again? Don't you understand? I've wrecked so many lives, left my child, destroyed Ken's love, made my parents and Ken's parents hate me. How can there be a new beginning after all that?"

The words came out of her like great clots of blood coughed up from the depths of her body—slowly, painfully, with perceptible pauses between each phrase. She went on, "You have no idea, Joe, what it means to hate yourself as much as I do. I'm no good to anybody, not to myself or to anyone else. I'm dirt, Joe, dirt! God, if you only knew all the dirty things I've done you'd never come to see me again."

"Nancy, there is one huge dimension you are forgetting."

"What's that?"

"God."

"What do you mean?" she asked, blank incomprehension in her eyes.

"Remember the cup you told me about in your dream? Nancy, that was the Lord's cup. It was His blood, the seal of His love for you. I believe that cup was in your dream because somewhere in your unconscious you were longing for the words you have heard me say when I lift up the cup during that service."

"I can't remember what they are."

I repeated them slowly, lovingly, "This cup is the new covenant in My blood, which is shed for the forgiveness of your sins."

Nancy covered her face with her hands and bent over with the sobbing pain of her life.

After a little while I said gently, "Nancy, the time has come to claim the promise of those words."

"I'm so stupid today, Joe. What do you mean?"

"I want you to stop trying to run your life yourself and let Jesus take over. I want you to be born afresh through His forgiveness. That's what new beginning means."

"I can't do it. I can't do it," she sobbed. Then she looked up at me in anger. "It's impossible, it's beyond me. And besides I don't deserve His love."

I stood up and said, "Let's not talk any more today, Nancy. You know I'll be back, don't you?"

The next two weeks were crucial. At each visit Nancy's mind seemed more clear. The odor of alcohol was omnipresent, but I couldn't be sure that it wasn't the effect of long saturation of her clothes, rugs, furniture. God's grace had kindled a faint, vulnerable light of hope in Nancy. I could see it in her eyes.

There was so much she wanted to talk about: Sally, her abuse of the child, her love of the child; past Christmases; the time Sally was baptized. And there was all the mess of her recent life: memories of men she could barely recall, places she could scarcely remember, horrible scenes which made her cry, Ken's rage and rejection.

By the end of the second week I knew something momentous was about to happen. The sun was even with us, shining golden and warm that day. Not even the grime on Nancy's windows could keep it out. As we sat down Nancy said the words I had waited so long to hear. "Joe, I'm ready."

"Ready for what, Nancy?" I wanted her to say it.

"I'm ready to make a new beginning. Ready to try to accept God's forgiveness."

I knelt on the floor before her and took her hands in mine. "Nancy, we'll try together. We have a long road ahead of us, but we can't lose because now we have outside help. With God on our side we can make it."

There followed a long period of prayer. At my bidding she did most of the praying. We prayed about Sally, about Ken, about the men with whom she had slept, at least those she could remember, about her guilt toward her daughter and her husband, about the pain she had brought to both their families. There was no part of her life during the previous few years for which she did not ask the Lord's forgiveness. There were not a few times when we had to stop and blow our noses.

Finally I felt the moment had come. I stood up, walked behind the sofa, placed my hands on her head and in the name of Jesus pronounced the forgiveness of God. Then I prayed that His love might fill her emptiness and empower her to do all that we had agreed to do.

That very afternoon she packed a small bag. It was the

beginning of a whole series of new, positive steps for Nancy. They didn't happen easily or quickly, but they happened. I telephoned Ken, then left for a hospital where I had arranged for her to be admitted to the clinic for the treatment of alcoholics. Before she returned home she had begun attending AA meetings, and this continued upon her discharge. She joined a prayer group for the nourishment of her life in Christ. Sally came back to her. Life was on course again.

As Nancy's greatest problem was in accepting forgiveness, Ken's greatest problem was in granting it. This made the recovery of the marriage a hard battle. I referred both Nancy and Ken to psychotherapists, and they gained invaluable insights from this experience.

But even after the layers of Ken's contributions to the problem had been defined, he was still bitter. He couldn't let matters rest. He was obsessive about the sexual betrayals. Nancy's new-found faith meant that she was under obligation to the truth, and Ken probed and probed for details of every past relationship he could dig up. He didn't seem able to put it down. He saw the misery he was causing, and he recognized with horror that he was even enjoying it.

I was petrified that Ken's obsessiveness would undo the gains Nancy had made. For weeks he would be free of his problem. Then he would bump into someone he thought she had been involved with and put her on the witness chair again. He confessed frankly to me that he and his therapist knew he was compulsively punishing Nancy. Clearly, another new beginning with Christ was needed.

And it was at this impasse in the relationship that Ken had the automobile accident. On a three-lane highway he swung into the left lane without being sure it was clear. Fortunately Ken was the only one hurt. His back was injured, putting him into the hospital in traction for seven weeks.

Nancy was now beyond the reach of his vengefulness and in the interim she blossomed.

During those weeks Ken and I talked at length about his problem. He knew he needed to be free of the bitter rage which haunted him, and at last there came a time when, like Nancy, he was ready.

It was about nine o'clock in the evening. Visiting hours were over. I grabbed the sweet opportunity of quietness while we had it.

"Ken, Nancy seems better these days than I think I've ever known her."

"It's true, Joe, I see it too. Today when she came through that door, all smiles, I didn't think I had ever seen her so beautiful."

"It's as though a light had turned on inside her, isn't it?"

"Inside and out," Ken replied, looking up at the steel rods which supported the traction ropes.

"I hope she stays that way after you get home." It was a plea more than a statement.

"Isn't there some way to make sure? God knows what I've put her through is worse than what she put me through. She didn't know what she was doing most of the time. I do. I feel like the scum of the earth."

"How long have you felt that way, Ken?"

"Ever since I've been in the hospital."

"If you really want to be different, Ken, there's a way."

"What's that?"

"Forgiveness. That's what makes new beginnings possible."

There was silence between us as I waited for Ken to digest this thought.

"We've talked about that before, Joe, and do you know I don't think until this minute I have been really ready to do it? It's time to quit the injured husband act, isn't it?"

"Are you truly ready to quit it?"

"I just told you, Joe, we've all suffered enough."

"Then this is a holy hour, Ken."

I got up, closed the door of the room and there followed a prayer time in which I guided Ken through a path of penitence. It was hard for him. He is not able to express himself as Nancy is; but we kept plowing the furrow we had begun. He gave the Lord his jealousy, his remembered violence toward Nancy, his sick pursuit of details of Nancy's past relations, his sin of unforgiveness.

When it was over I claimed the forgiveness of Christ for him as I had done for Nancy and pled with the Lord Jesus to fill him with His love.

We both felt the peace in that room. "Joe, you've been telling me many times that God is for me, wanting to set me free, giving me new chances, and now I know what you mean."

We smiled at each other. He knew and I knew in one of those mysterious certainties of the spirit that the burden of his guilt and rage was gone. The power of sin had been broken. Their lives and their marriage had come to a new beginning.

Chapter 2

How Do We Know?

How DO WE know that God is for us? By what authority do I claim that He is forever drawing us to new and positive beginnings? The authority of experience is one way—experience such as Nancy's and Ken's, experience present and past, personal and collective. But experience is not the only source Christians must consult.

For us the authority of Scripture is essential. The first threshold of Holy Writ over which I stepped into the presence of the living Christ was through the doorway of St. John's Gospel. It has ever since been my dwelling place. I have gone out of that abode to the riches of the other Gospels, to the plumbless depths of the Epistles, to the incomparable love affair between God and His people recorded in the Old Testament, but always I come back to my first home: the Gospel of John.

I humbly join the company of those scholars who believe the figure behind those writings is none other than the disciple whom Jesus loved, dictating in his old age the distillation of all he had seen and heard as a young man and all he had learned through his subsequent travels. The authority of his Gospel is conclusive for me, upholding the authority of Scripture from Genesis to Revelation.

In his final sentence, St. John refers to the staggering and voluminous material available about Jesus. And yet, of all the miracles of healing he must have witnessed, he records only four. I have often wondered why he selected those four. Each miracle, I saw at the outset, illustrates the basic message of the fourth Gospel: each proclaims that God is present in His world. But as I have reflected through the years on these four healing instances, they seem to me to illustrate something further. He is not only present, they tell me, but He is for us—offering new beginnings in Him whenever we come to the end of our own resources.

Think of the nobleman whose son lies ill at Capernaum. He is a man accustomed to power. It is not his habit to plead for help—especially not from a lowly carpenter when he himself is an official of the royal court! Social divisions in the time of Jesus were clearly defined, and one did not cross them lightly. Yet in spite of all that money and position can buy, the nobleman's son remains "at the point of death." In desperation the father seeks out a wandering healer whose fame has reached his ears.

The remarkable note in the story is the man's confidence in Jesus from the moment they meet. And, as always, Jesus responds to trust. What was there in the encounter which told the nobleman so unmistakably that Jesus was for him? Why was there no shadow of doubt or guilt to darken his faith? I wonder if it wasn't something he saw in the eyes of Jesus? Haven't you ever met a person of wide reputation and looked him squarely in the eye, only to have something click in your head? It was no rational process which produced the click. An intuition told you, "This person is real. He is the person he appears to be. I can trust him. He is authentic."

Might not the nobleman have had a similar experience? Is it not likely that the steadfast gaze of Jesus, fixed so firmly on the nobleman, persuaded him to give his heart entirely to the man of Galilee? Something in the eyes of Jesus told the anxious father in front of him, "I care for you. I want a new beginning for you and your son."

So the nobleman pled for the life of his sick child. And at the word of Jesus the son was healed. In gratitude and praise, St. John tells us, the nobleman "and his whole household" henceforward followed Jesus. It was a new beginning not only for a dying boy but for a whole family.

Or think of the man born blind. Everyone, disciples as well as neighbors, seems to know this beggar of Jerusalem. His blindness is common knowledge. Then Jesus arrives, anoints his eyes in an ancient ritual, and tells him to wash in the pool of Siloam. The Gospel records that he "went and washed and came [back] seeing."

How does this man dare to do exactly as Jesus instructs him? What makes him obey the Master so readily? Why is there no resistance? The Pharisees have assured him his condition is the result of sin. For centuries people have believed illness to be a form of divine punishment. The disciples think the same. They ask Jesus who sinned, the man or his parents?

What made the blind man dare to go against this timeless, appalling linkage between physical affliction and guilt? Why did he obey the Lord in spite of all he had been taught? He had never heard, as he said, "since the world began," of anyone who opened the eyes of one born blind. What made him dare to tread such dangerous waters? There was every reason to expect disappointment. No one around him shared his hope. How did he find the resources of faith to look to Jesus for a new beginning?

I wonder if it could have been the voice of the Master. Clearly His was a special voice. After Mary found the empty tomb she thought the man in the garden was the gardener until Jesus spoke. I wonder if the man born blind might not have caught a quality of immeasurable compassion in the voice of the Nazarene: "Neither hath this man sinned, nor his parents." Might not the love behind that voice have aroused an unspeakable excitement in the man? He would obey that voice anywhere, anytime.

Through this miracle, Jesus put the axe to the intractable feeling that sickness is divine judgment, certain proof that God is against us. It is amazing how persistent this idea is in our experience. I have known people who were convinced their evil thoughts or misdeeds brought on a serious illness. Doubtless there is a connection between our health and the way we live our lives. Sin and the resulting guilt possess genuine power to cripple our physical bodies. But that is not God's intention nor is it His responsibility if we misuse our freedom to abuse our health and wreck our lives. If illness becomes a consequence of such misconduct, let us put the burden of it where it belongs—on our own shoulders, not on God. His will is always to win us back to wholeness, to sweep away the past and provide us with ever-new beginnings.

But in the case of the man born blind, no such misconduct was at issue. Jesus did not look for an explanation in the life of the beggar nor in the lives of his parents. Instead, He saw it as a part of the dark tragedy of human experience. More, it was an opportunity to give glory to God and to identify Himself as the "Light of the world" which the darkness is powerless to overcome. It was a demonstration that though some cherished souls come into this world with severe handicaps and limitations, God is nonetheless for us, bringing hope that even in these tragic situations new beginnings are possible.

Then there was the healing of the crippled man at the pool of Bethesda. Archeology has unearthed this pool and it tallies precisely with the description in St. John's Gospel. When the angel of healing hovered above its soft, murmuring surface, the first person to touch the waters was healed. This man had lain for 38 years waiting for the crucial moments of angelic visitation, but when they came someone else always reached the poolside ahead of him.

Thirty-eight years is almost a whole working life today. I wonder how many times this man struggled toward those healing waters? After countless attempts must he not have concluded that God was against him? When others were healed, how did he feel? How could he have avoided the ravages of self-pity? After 38 years he must surely have thought, "Everyone else gets a blessing, but I never do. Others obtain God's mercy, but I am never among the favored ones. There must be something wrong with me, since neither men nor God make a move to help me."

Possibly, too, after so many years of disappointment he may have found it convenient to cling to his illness. He might have said to himself, "I may as well content myself with my infirmity and get as much mileage out of it as I can. At least it provides me with a lot of sympathy. I'm used to it now, and without it I'd have to learn all over again to take responsibility."

Then one day something happens to change all this. Jesus sees him by the Sheep Gate pool in Jerusalem. Learning how long this man has lain by these mysterious waters, the Master asks a pointed question which goes to the heart of the man's condition of despair and resentment: "Do you want to be healed?" Instead of answering, the sick man begins to complain: "I have no man to put me into the pool when the water is troubled, and while I am going another steps down before me."

Jesus makes no further inquiries; he knows the man better than the man knows himself. He issues a straightforward command. "Rise, take up your pallet, and walk." And in that instant the man is healed. More than the witness of eyes and ears, something in the deepest core of the invalid has heard Truth emanating from the Man before him, and has responded to it.

How different are these three healing miracles, yet how consistent is the life-giving figure behind them! One miracle involves the profoundest ties of love, such as those between father and child, which bind us to one another; another touches upon the darkest mystery of our lives, the tragedy of abysmal suffering which comes to us through no one's fault; the third bears upon the complexity of illness, its participation in the perversity of life and the strange mixtures of motivation which often complicate our sicknesses.

And there you have it all: illness which can deprive us of those we love, illness which baffles the heart because of its injustice and illness which participates in the inconsistencies of our being. To all these conditions, John's Gospel brings the good news that Christ is always and forever able to provide new beginnings.

There is, however, one other healing selected by St. John for our reflection. It is, of course, the raising of Lazarus.

From various textual references, we surmise that the home in Bethany where Lazarus lived with his sisters, Mary and Martha, was a special place to Jesus. Most of the time the Master, unlike "the foxes of the fields and the birds of the air," had "nowhere to lay his head." But in Bethany, it was always a homecoming.

Out of the intimacy which Jesus shared with this household in Bethany there springs a noble confession. It is like
an arrow going to the target of John's Gospel. Martha de-
clares it. Her beloved brother has been dead four days.
Yet in the face of this ultimate tragedy her words breathe
her unshaken confidence in the love and purpose of Jesus.
When she learns that Jesus has returned to Judea, she rushes
to meet him: "Lord, if you had been here, my brother would
not have died. And even now I know that whatever you
ask from God, God will give you." It is a precursor of Paul's
shout of victory, "If God be for us, who can be against
us!"

The Lord goes to where Lazarus is buried.

And there, when the stone is moved from the mouth
of the tomb, Jesus calls Lazarus to come forth. A life which
was finished begins again.

No greater miracle of healing is recorded in the Gospels
than this one. Once more St. John is telling us that in spite
of the most appalling appearances to the contrary, including
even death itself, the Savior is unfailingly for us, holding
out new beginnings even when it seems the final hope has
fled. For some it was His eyes that gave courage to believe
this, for others His voice or His penetrating knowledge of
their own depths. For Martha it was long, proven, intimate,
personal experience. For us all, however we come to know
Him, the message is always of unquenchable love which
extends even beyond the grave.

There are many other ways in which I could support
the theme of this book from the authority of Scripture,
but I have chosen the healing miracles recorded in St. John's
Gospel because that book is the home of my soul. I have
pondered its texts while eating and walking, while rising
up and sitting down. I have found its passages in my dreams.
I feel confident I shall have no difficulty in recognizing the

beloved disciple when I finally meet him face to face in the next sphere of life which God has prepared for those who return His love. I dare to hope at the instant of my death St. John might say to me, "You see, the Lord has been for you too, all along." Whereupon I shall be content to fall on my face in overwhelming gratitude.

When I say Jesus is for us, I mean He is for us, shadows and all. When we make a mess of our lives, He is for us. When the sin and tragedy of life draw us into the pit of self-hatred, often taking everyone we can touch with us, He is still for us, straining His eyes to see us returning to the Father's house where alone we can fulfill His everlasting purpose. When sickness afflicts our bodies and souls, our thinking and feeling, He is for us, ready to heal us, restore us, or reunite us to Himself beyond the body of this life. The impotent, the blind, the lame, the dying—He is for all of us, in every circumstance holding out to us the possibilities of new and abundant life.

As I lift my eyes to the mountain peaks on the horizon still glistening white with snow and listen to St. Martin's bells ringing the changes of the noon hour, spreading their solemn signature over this fair earth, I think this spinning globe is the antechamber of the Father's house. Why do we misuse it and pretend we own it? Why can't we honor this lovely earth, knowing it has sprung from the cosmic void at God's command to provide a home for us all? What greater evidence than the world around us do we need that God is eternally for us?

When I was a child, I divided my time between village and farm. It was something surpassing wonderful to watch the men milking cows, pulling each teat strongly and deftly, now and then squirting a thin, white stream toward the mouth of one of the barn cats. I can still hear the rhythmic

spurt of the milk when it first hits the empty pail. One
of my greatest joys was to rise early and accompany Uncle
Jim on his journey to town with the full milk cans, his
aged, white-dappled horse, Rose, hitched to the wagon.
In the predawn grayness I sat close to Uncle Jim, a man
of few words, while in silence we rumbled our way over
the dirt road, and Rose left her steaming manure in our
wake. Village folk could set their clocks by us, hearing the
steel-rimmed wagon wheels clattering over the cobblestones
as we came to town.

Then there was haying time. I was neither large enough
nor strong enough to be of much help, but I could stand
in the wagon into which others pitched the fresh-smelling
hay and, with pitchfork in hand, spread it about in order
to obtain a maximum load. When we got to the barn I
would hop from the top of the strawy load and begin the
task of distributing the hay in the barn loft as I had done
in the wagon. It was a dusty business, but the shouts and
laughter of the men made it exciting, and I blissfully knew
that Aunt Hetty would have a steaming meal waiting for
us when the dinner bell rang.

The nights, oh, how I loved the nights. I went to bed
with the sun. The guinea hens lined up in a straight row
on the rooftop of the barn, making their eerie, clucking
sounds, protesting the dying of the light. But it was not
their voices I listened for. It was the voice of the whippoor-
will. The last sound I remembered before the dip of sleep
was his patient, persistent call.

I was always sad when summer was over, and I had to
go back to live in the village. The rhythm of nature with
its endlessly renewed beginnings; the procession of planting,
growing, harvesting; the moist generativity of the earth;
the coinciding of the daily routine with the rising and setting
of the sun, combined to produce in me a nameless joy and

an indestructible security. It never occurred to me as I watched Uncle Jim bow his head over his folded hands at mealtime, that God was not boundlessly for us. Our daily life and God's will for us were one. Each morning was a fresh beginning; each day we danced anew to the quiet, deep music of His providence.

To be sure, these are memories of a child. I now know there were anxieties and dark potentialities for evil even in that beloved household. But I didn't know those things then. I only knew I was wrapped in a mantle of love, God's love and the love of family.

I wonder if St. John's childhood bore even the faintest resemblance to those halcyon summer days of my childhood. Somehow I think there is a connection. Might not St. John have felt such a natural childlike trust in the God of Abraham, Isaac and Jacob in his earliest years, sensing Him in the earth, the stars, the hearthfire of his home, and then finding it the most natural thing in the world to transfer that trust to the Master? I think the roots of his loyalty and faith were deeply embedded in his being.

How else did it happen that he was the only disciple to share those last hours of the cross? Nothing could shake St. John's confidence, not even his Lord's apparent defeat in the agony and humiliation of crucifixion. Nor was it any accident that St. John was the first to reach the empty tomb, outrunning St. Peter. I wonder what his thoughts were as he ran? My intuition tells me they were of this character: "It has happened just as He promised it would! He isn't dead. He's alive!" Doubtless St. John was wonderstruck when the angel told him, "He is not here. He is risen." However, I think out of the depths of his being, St. John knew what to expect. The angel's pronouncement was confirmation for St. John, not revelation. It was the final seal on the beloved disciple's trust.

Now Jesus was for him not only in all the naturalness he had previously known but with the resurrection, St. John grasped that Jesus was for him and for all people, beyond time, beyond space, beyond human knowing. Easter was, once for all, the conclusive evidence that new beginnings are not just possible with God but part of the Divine Nature Himself. My experience may suggest this, other people's may confirm it; it is Scripture which tells me for certain that it is so.

Chapter 3

Taking Hold of the Rail

BUT HOW DO WE get this wonderful knowledge from the head to the pit of the stomach? It happens, I am convinced, precisely during those black periods of our lives when, at the outset, God seems farthest away.

I recall such a time in my own life. It was shortly after World War II. There was no program to help ex-chaplains like myself resettle in the parish ministry, and for many months I was jobless. Finally, an old church with a dwindling membership, located in a depressed area of Albany, New York, called me to be their pastor.

I was at the end of my rope in every way. The responsibility of our first child fell like an avalanche about my head, though I loved our baby daughter enormously. But my wife Carola, months after childbirth, was still coping unsuccessfully with severe depression. On Sunday mornings I faced a congregation of less than 150 people in a sanctuary built to seat almost a thousand. It was Neo-Gothic with beautifully carved, dark woodwork and a U-shaped balcony running down both sides and across the back. I never saw it fully occupied. The pulpit was located beneath the organ, making visual contact between most of the congregation and me difficult. On Sundays I used to look around at those empty pews, cushioned in faded damask, and be overwhelmed by a sense of utter inadequacy and a nameless terror.

Then there was the business of "parish calling," something which today is like a piece of cake to me. But at that time it was a horror. I can remember driving my second-hand, black Dodge to an address of some parishioner and sitting in the parked car, paralyzed with fear, my shirt soaked with perspiration. Sometimes I made it and sometimes I didn't. Occasionally, I would get as far as the doorbell only to turn and flee, hating myself all the way.

Nor can I forget Frances Hughson. She had been a missionary to China and later married one of Albany's lumber barons. Mr. Hughson had been dead many years, leaving his fortune to his wife. There were no children. I was informed early in my ministry there that she was the church's largest contributor, so naturally I was to treat her with extreme care. God only knows the psychic pain thousands of pastors carry in order not to offend their "largest contributor."

Frances Hughson's judgment on all matters was decisive. If the social hall needed recarpeting, she made the decision. If the furnace had to be repaired, she was consulted. If the organist's salary was to be increased, she footed the bill. Committees were convened, others were asked for their opinions, but everyone knew that ultimately Mrs. Hughson called the tune.

I became paranoid about the woman. She had an eccentric manner of breaking into a smile at the most unlikely moments, and when I saw her bespectacled, ash-white face twist into that crooked grin at some perfectly solemn passage in the sermon, I almost quit on the spot. I used to have Walter Mitty fantasies in which my powers of invective were unlimited. Her house was full of priceless ivory, porcelain, rugs and tapestries brought from China, and one of my favorite fantasies involved heavy sarcasm regarding the image of selfless sacrifice she liked to project from her missionary days.

I am now certain that my hostility toward this woman, long since dead, was quite unjustified, but I didn't know it at the time. All I knew then was that it was a part of my overall misery, like the headaches and nausea, which were daily trials to be borne.

One Saturday night I was in the sanctuary alone, reading my sermon aloud, standing at the pulpit. The only light in the place came from a half-opened door to the vestibule by which I had entered the church and from the pulpit light on my manuscript. All of a sudden I began to shake physically. Try as I might, I couldn't stop trembling. I let myself fall to the carpet behind the pulpit, and I vaguely remember calling out the name of Christ: "Jesus, Jesus help me; Jesus, Jesus help me." Faces passed before my eyes, faces of young soldiers I had buried at sea and in the ground, faces of wounded men, faces of my childhood, Frances Hughson's face.

I couldn't possibly estimate how long this went on. At last some form of total exhaustion took over and I lay silent, not knowing what to do next. Then I heard a "whisper." I don't know to this day how to explain it in natural terms. The only way I can fathom it now, as I did then, is in supernatural terms. A voice softly spoke to me in that nearly dark sanctuary. I believed then, as I believe now, that it was the voice of the Lord. He said, "Take my yoke upon you and learn of me, for my yoke is easy and my burden is light."

I was stunned. There was no question in my mind about the objective reality of that message. I had not simply summoned it from memory. As I lay there I could feel my weakness, which had amounted to immobility, being transformed into strength. Presently I knew I had enough power to stand, and I pulled myself up by the ledges of the pulpit. I stood there leaning my weight on it while I felt a warm flow of strength engulf my being. It was unmistakable. God was present in this place, and—more astonishingly—He was for me! He willed to help me. He desired health for me. His wish was to restore me to my rightful mind, to release me from the intense anxiety and depression threatening my sanity. He cared for those I loved as much as I cared for them. My burden was as nothing compared to His burden for the salvation of the world, and He called his burden light! What I needed more than anything else was to give myself to this loving God. If I could only trust Him, He would give me the power to begin again.

All of this is far more rationally articulated now than it was then, but the essence is the same. I knew the Savior had saved *me*. I *felt* the depth of His caring.

After this momentous experience, I began to be able to think more clearly and objectively about what was going on in my life. I have never labored under the illusion that any of us are self-made. One of the ways in which God shows His love is that in the crises of life, He always provides just the right person to see us through, if only we have sense enough and humility enough to look around and find him or her. Albany is a short distance from Pittsfield, and there I found Dr. Austin Riggs, to whose skill, time, wisdom, and compassion I shall be forever indebted.

Nor did this great pioneer in psychotherapy ever minimize the depth of my experience of Christ in the dark of the church that night. He was not a reductionist. He did not try to psychologize the experience. He called it by its right name: "A breakthrough of the spirit," a new beginning in Christ.

The Lord of course had been for me all along, in neurosis as well as health. And from Bible reading and seminary training I understood with my mind that this must be so. I didn't feel it "in my guts" though—not the way I felt the terror and the inadequacy—until this experience brought me quite literally to my knees. I have wondered since if this is one reason that God "permits" crises in our lives: to bring His love alive in our experience.

I recall another very different kind of crisis when His supportive caring became a gut-level reality. It happened in Hattiesburg, Mississippi. After the Voters Rights Bill was passed in the early 1960s, many of us went south to help black people register to vote.

I had a car, and my assignment was to go out to the villages surrounding Hattiesburg, explain the new legislation to such folk as I could find and drive them to the courthouse. This meant first cracking the crust of fear many black people harbored in their hearts. I also had to accompany the registrants into the courthouse and stand by while they responded to simple questions of age and residency, in such marked contrast to the days when difficult parts of the Constitution, in fine print, were pushed before them with a peremptory command to read aloud. Here was a new beginning indeed, a radical departure from the past, and like all such departures, accompanied by pain.

One elderly man rises vividly from my memory of those days. He was so crippled with arthritis he could barely walk even with a cane. Several of his teeth were missing and he was bald save for a white fringe around his head. He was fairly tall so it was easy for him to put one hand on my shoulder, and with support from his cane on the other side, we managed. He hadn't been to Hattiesburg for several years, as he had no car.

His wife, though equally old, was able-bodied and worked as a domestic in some home to which she walked every morning, leaving at 6 A.M. Their home was simple, barren of all the appliances we take for granted. But to my eyes it was somehow beautiful. Though outwardly there was no resemblance, inwardly it had the grace and simplicity of a monastery. I slept in their living room while I was in their village.

After we were parked in Hattiesburg as near the courthouse as possible, we shuffled our way toward the steps leading to the county clerk's office. I hadn't realized I was escorting a well-known personage.

"Hey, William, where do you think you're goin'?"

"That nigger-lover gonna to show you where to put your X, William?"

But up we went, my friend's face absolutely expressionless. All his energies, seemingly, were fixed on getting from one step to the next.

Inside, the man behind the registration desk looked up. "For Gawd's sake, William, where in hell did you come from?"

"Came to get registered to vote."

There were the usual uncomplimentary remarks. But presently, there it was in large, clear, if somewhat shaky, script, "William Potter."

We got up and returned the way we came, past the gibes and averted faces. I could never get white people to meet my eyes during those days in Hattiesburg. There was no difficulty in sensing their resentment, and I did not condemn them, for change doesn't come easily to me either, and change is what new beginning is all about.

All the way back to the village we were followed by a car in which two men were riding, wearing police caps and badges. I knew from experience I must drive very slowly, meticulously obeying every possible traffic regulation. His street at last. The car which had slowly tailed us all the way back went off at breakneck speed as we pulled over to the tiny Potter household.

After we got out of the car and were inside the house, William Potter put his arms around me and wept. I think they were the holiest arms I have ever felt.

"Thank you, Jesus; thank you, Jesus; thank you, Jesus," was all he said as he bowed over me.

When I had made us each a cup of coffee on his wood stove, he said it again, "Thank you, Jesus."

All I could say was, "Without Him, we would never have made it, would we?"

"Never, never in a million years," he answered.

"Thank you, Jesus," we both prayed.

He was for us! And what was best, we both knew it in a new way. William Potter had taken a risk, had dared a new beginning, and in this exigency had gotten the truth of Christ into his bones.

One day, years ago, I went to the top of the Eiffel Tower in Paris. Unlike the top of the Empire State Building in Manhattan, you have a sense of precariousness there. The walls are not so high, nor are you wholly screened in as you are in New York. For the first time I had some sense of the pattern of Paris as I let my eyes rove in all directions. There was Notre Dame, the Seine River, the Arc de Triomphe, the different suburban segments. Then I looked directly down from that dizzying height, and my hands gripped tightly the railing before me. I was thankful for its firmness. I was grateful for its protection. I knew without it my life could have been shattered in seconds. All the way down in the elevator I thought about that railing. I said to myself, *The Lord is like that railing. He can be depended on.* Then I thought with terror, *Suppose I didn't know that? How would I find out? How would I grasp that unfailing support?*

Not long ago a young mother named Mary sat in my study sharing with me the pain and confusion of her life. At the end of the hour we prayed together, invoking God's strength for her struggle. Tearfully she asked, "But, Joe, how am I to hang on until my appointment with you next week?"

"You do it one hour at a time, Mary," I replied. "Compose your spirit in quietness, fold your hands and say, 'Thank you, Lord Jesus. I know You are the answer. You have never failed to give me the strength I needed when I asked for it in the past, and I know You will not fail me now.' "

I had given her a railing to grab hold of. It is the railing I have used all my life. I only wish I didn't have to use it so often lest I outlive God's patience with me.

When Mary came to see me the following week I was not surprised to hear her say, "It works!" Like the railing on the Eiffel Tower, God was there. He is always "able to keep you from falling, and to present you faultless before the presence of His glory with exceeding joy." In this crisis time of her life Mary had reached for that Divine Support, and now she knows in a way her mind alone could never have arrived at, that Jesus is for *her*, Mary, even as we grope together toward a beginning that still seems impossibly far off.

Chapter 4

Sin

FEW THINGS PLEASE me so much as to have people come into my study, look around and exclaim, "My, what a nice room: I don't know why, but I feel safe in here." Or: "I feel so relaxed here I could stay all day."

It is not a large room, and three sides lined with bookshelves make it smaller still. Here and there among the books are objects people have given me over the years: a model of a sailboat made by a patient in a mental hospital as a token of our faith that he could be healed; a bronze statue of St. Francis given me by the son of a man whom I helped to die in peace. There are growing plants, an Oriental rug, two red overstuffed wing chairs, an old mantle clock with a charming chime, a wooden desk, two leaded-glass windows looking out toward the southern sky.

Something in the intimate atmosphere touches a deep place in the need people bring to that space. I am also certain that the amount of prayer which goes on in that room is by now a palpable presence.

Naturally one of the new beginnings which people most often come here seeking is a fresh start on a marriage that has gone sour. Here in metropolitan New York we are told that the divorce rate is now one out of two marriages. What is happening to us?

I am never one to feel comfortable with simplistic answers. The question is endlessly complex, and therefore the answers are assuredly complex. The disciplines of psychology, sociology, economics—all have their roles to play in defining the problem as well as the solution. However, religion has its unique contribution to make as well. Religion alone can bring us to the point of genuine new beginning, for religion alone can speak to us about sin.

Sin is a word in our vocabulary which has had a bad press. For many people it produces an automatic block in communication, while others distort its meaning by restricting it to a few areas of behavior.

But I believe we must take up the word again, because no other quite describes our situation. To the Old Testament Hebrew "sin" meant that magnetlike inner force which perpetually draws us away from the target of our true selves toward rebellion, enmity, willfulness and self-centeredness. The earliest memory which expressed this perverse rebellion against our own good is the story of the Garden of Eden: the apple, the snake and the tree of knowledge. It was the way the Hebrew people expressed their awareness of the tragic elements in life.

Our generation is at a greater loss to conceptualize this dimension of reality than were our forebears. Because we have no operative story or explanation or symbol with which to contemplate our experience of evil, we are left with nothing but despair. The media are full of helplessness. Remember *Catch 22* and *A Clockwork Orange* and *Johnny Got His Gun?* More recently the Italian film maker, Bunuel, told the story of an older man's obsession with a younger woman. The film ends with a senseless, terroristic tactic in which they are both accidentally blown up by a bomb. And now the books written after Vietnam are becoming films, bringing back to all of us the tragic vision of American power separated from truth. Despair is the sickness of this decade.

How could it be otherwise in an age of gargantuan violence when we have no symbols, no truth, no concepts of tragedy to explain ourselves to ourselves? Christians have dared to look at this deep-seated perversity and call it sin. In the first epistle of John we are told: "If we say that we have no sin, we deceive ourselves, and the truth is not in us."

By sin I understand that to mean the destructiveness we all display in our lives, even under the veneer of high motives. Sin is the racist receiving the sacrament of holy communion while his church door is barred to men of another race. It is the person obsessed with sexual conquest, defending his activity as "natural." It is the company executive who puts the profit motive ahead of the interests of human beings. It is the son or daughter who professes how much he loves his parents, yet continually brings them sorrow through irresponsible behavior. It is parents who avow their devotion to their children but refuse to be truly available to them. It is the person who thinks that this fair earth—its air, water and natural resources—belong to him instead of to God. Within the listening walls of my study it is so often the husband or wife who professes commitment to the marriage but will not make sacrifices for the welfare of the partner.

Let us go at the problem another way. Sin is not only present when we lie or deliberately deceive one another. Lies can be forgiven. It is when we no longer honor truth

itself as a universal norm to which we have a fundamental
obligation. Sin is not only found in the structures of an
unjust society in which 40 percent of young blacks cannot
find employment. Sooner or later inescapable social pres-
sures will compel some accommodation. Sin is most deeply
present when we become impervious to the majesty of justice itself, refusing to bow beneath its requirements of respect for the rights of all people. Sin is not only when
we betray someone we love and misuse the emotional vul-
nerability of others. Betrayal, though unspeakably painful,
can be healed. Sin is when we no longer revere love itself
as the humanizing force of life.

What does this add up to? Sin is the refusal to allow
the living God to reach us. It is life without repentance
and therefore without the possibility of new beginnings.
It is turning our backs instead of our faces to God's beckon-
ing love when He invites us to new vistas of hope and
renewal.

If this is our problem, what is the answer?

I find it laid out most clearly in the parable of the prodigal
son. You remember how the story ends. "But while he was
yet at a distance, his father saw him and had compassion,
and ran and embraced him and kissed him." The elder son
protests against this unconditional forgiveness without punishment or penalty. But the father knows that his rebellious
son has been grievously punished already, cutting himself
off from all that was good and true. The father perceives
the suffering, the shame, the self-hatred, the agonized confusion which the prodigal son has experienced until he was
sick unto death. The father understands the fearful alone-
ness in which his son has lived, cut off from the place
where he truly belongs.

Clearly it is the story of every one of us. We cut ourselves
off from the heavenly Father's rule in our lives, determining

to go it alone, until some calamity of life catches up with us. Then, if we have a grain of grace left in us, we will arise and return to the Father whose love waits for us, prepared to do for us above all that we could ask or think.

Suppose the prodigal son had never repented. Suppose he had never said, "I have sinned"; suppose he had never permitted the truth of his condition to have reached him. There would have been no reunion. The lost would have remained lost. The dead would have remained dead. There would have been no chance for a new beginning with his father.

And this is our tragedy and our sin: that so often we fail to respond to the inner voice which whispers, "I will arise and go to my father," where alone we can find the fresh sources of our life.

I was forced to face this dark reality with special intensity when I became involved in the lives of two fascinating people. They were both European. He had been brought up in Western Germany, she was born and raised in Cornish England. They met in London where Virginia had obtained a job in an investment house following her training in the London School of Economics. Pieder was stationed in England by his company.

Virginia had the loveliest golden hair I think I ever saw. It glistened in the sunlight like a crown. No one who ever knew her failed to comment on its beauty. She had blue-green eyes, a somewhat dumpy figure anchored in solid square-heeled shoes, and the usual healthy English complexion.

This daughter of a Cornwall architect was brilliant beyond all normal expectations. Within 18 months, the investment firm in which she worked as an analyst knew they had a prize.

As her star of competence was rising in her firm, she

met Pieder. He was typically German: tall, inward-looking, dark-haired, urbane, a model of efficiency and decision, unbendable as iron when once he had formed his opinions.

They were married in St. George's Church in London. I never knew much about their first few years of marriage save that they were filled with problems. They had moved to New York after Pieder had been put in charge of one of his company's large American operations. Virginia had easily found a new position in an investment house on Wall Street. We met in late autumn at a dinner party in the apartment of a mutual friend named Norma.

"I'm an executive of a company based in Bonn. Now tell me, what do you do?" Pieder asked in a deeply pleasant German voice employing that universal opener of all western societies.

"I'm a clergyman."

"You're the first minister we've met in America," Virginia exclaimed in British university accents.

"Then," I said quite innocently, "you must have recently come to this country."

"I'm afraid not," Virginia said somewhat embarrassedly. "We've been in Manhattan four years, but we never go to church, though I pop in at St. Thomas' every so often for an organ recital."

We were interrupted then, but at coffee time, Virginia came over to the crowded sofa where I was sitting, took a pillow from somewhere and seated herself at my feet. I glanced up from my coffee and saw Pieder a few feet away engaged in conversation but looking at us with frowning disapproval.

From somewhere in Virginia's depths I sensed a feeling of desperation. It was evident in the frightened way in which she looked to see where Pieder was. She came almost breathlessly to her object.

"I have heard about you from Norma. May I come to see you?"

I saw Pieder moving toward us so I said rapidly, shifting my position to get up and bending toward Virginia, "Ask Norma for my telephone number and call me for an appointment."

She phoned the next day and before long we were meeting once a week in my book-lined study. As I suspected, the problem was her marriage. The crucial interview came several months after we had begun. She had grown dreadfully thin.

"Joe, I can't trust him anymore. He lies to me about everything. He treats me more and more like a servant. When he wants sex, it is at his convenience, and it's all over in minutes. There is no tenderness between us, and yet if I'm even a few minutes late getting home from work, he's insane with jealousy."

She paused, adding, "I don't think I can go on any longer. I haven't the strength to fight him anymore."

"Can't we arrange to see a doctor about this weight loss of yours?" I asked.

"You know how Pieder is about doctors. He thinks they're only out for his money and with intelligence anyone can take care of his own health. Besides," she added, "you remember what a wild harangue I went through when I told him I had come to see you, and you had recommended psychotherapy for both of us."

"Why do you suppose he tolerates your visits to me, Virginia?"

"Oh," Virginia said, her eyes avoiding mine while she turned her lovely shining head toward the mantlepiece clock, "he thinks you're harmless because you're a pastor."

The weeks went on. Virginia's thinness became alarming. The trip to my office exhausted her; consequently, we began holding our sessions in their elegant East Side apartment with its splendid view of the mid-Manhattan bridge. There were books in German and English on the bookshelves, Dresden china objects in a glass case, a round table covered with a tapestry rug in place of the typical American coffee table, French Impressionist prints on the walls.

By this time it was May, and I was determined to have a confrontation with Pieder about Virginia's health. There was no one else to do it. Virginia refused to tell her family about her problems, and she had no close friends in America. Something had to be done. Every visit I made that spring alarmed me more. Her weight was down to 88 pounds. Her hair had lost its sheen. She talked with slow, stuttering speech as though every word was an effort. She had resigned her job. She conserved all her energy to prepare Pieder's evening meal when he was home, but nothing was ever satisfactory to him, and he was absent more and more frequently. Her loneliness was abysmal.

So we agreed on a day and an hour when I could talk to Pieder. I waited with her for him to come home from work. Virginia was intensely agitated, her distended eyes darting from side to side, her frail figure literally trembling. Her hands moved constantly, fingering the edges of the sweater which drooped loosely from her shoulders. At 6:50 P.M. we heard Pieder's key in the door lock of the apartment. A look of utter terror came over Virginia's face.

"What is this?" demanded Pieder with fierce angry eyes. "It's not quite time to make the funeral arrangements, is it?"

"Pieder," I said as gently as I could, "please sit down. We have a lot to talk about."

"Is this really appropriate?" asked Pieder, still towering above both of us where we sat on the sofa, Virginia's thin body lost in its capaciousness. "What goes on between my wife and myself and the decisions I choose to make about our lives are strictly private. I see no reason to admit an intrusion."

I could see that his hands were gripped behind his back as he turned toward Virginia, "What is he doing here? Did you invite him?"

Virginia was wholly incapable of responding.

"No, Pieder, I invited myself."

"Well, then get out!" he bellowed as he turned the full fury of his madness on me.

"Very well, Pieder, if you refuse to sit down and talk things over rationally, I shall call the police and take Virginia with me. All that is required is her permission."

With barely controlled rage he asked, "And just what do you propose doing with my wife?"

"I propose taking her to the hospital, Pieder."

"Oh, so that's it!" cried Pieder triumphantly as though he had found the key he had been searching for.

He continued, "I suppose you think you are going to lock her up in some state mental hospital, or maybe you're prepared to meet the expenses of Payne-Whitney?" This last was said with heavy sarcasm, referring to a well-known private hospital for psychiatric care in New York.

"I have no such intentions at all, Pieder. Virginia doesn't need a psychiatric hospital, she needs a general hospital for medical diagnosis and treatment."

By now Pieder was striding up and down the room. As there seemed no point in further discussion, I said, "Virginia, where is the telephone?"

Pieder stopped stock-still, wheeled on me, and through clenched teeth muttered, "You wouldn't dare."

I said nothing but got up and walked toward the room to which Virginia was pointing. I felt Pieder's eyes fixed on me, and I knew he would probably strike me. So I turned to face him and by an authority not my own I said, "Pieder, in the name of Christ, sit down in that chair behind you, and don't move until I tell you to do so."

Like a balloon which is suddenly punctured he collapsed on the chair and covered his face with his hands.

Instead of moving to the phone I returned to the sofa. "Now, Pieder, listen to me. Virginia is desperately sick. If she goes on like this, she'll be dead before the summer is over. We've got to do something."

There was not a word from Pieder. His breathing was heavy. I couldn't tell what was going on in his head. We waited.

Finally, he said, "You can take her."

At Virginia's instructions I fetched a light coat and her handbag from her bedroom and we quickly left. Pieder never raised his head.

Virginia's condition was diagnosed as anorexia, a condition which affects the lungs, makes breathing difficult, eating almost impossible. Intravenous feeding improved her condition somewhat, but as the weeks went on it was clear that other vital functions of her body had been drastically affected. Pieder hardly ever visited her except occasionally on Saturday afternoons when he stayed no more than 10 or 15 minutes. They had nothing to say to one another.

One day I said to Virginia, "Why didn't you leave him long ago?"

"I've asked myself that question a hundred times lying here in this hospital room. It's all very complicated. I stare at the ceiling and these bare, green walls and thank God I'm not in that apartment anymore."

When Virginia recovered she moved into a studio apartment on the West Side, vastly relieved that her firm took her back into their employ. Her commitment to the marriage was profound. In spite of all she had experienced of Pieder's cruelty, she was eager to try again. But by this time, Pieder had found someone else.

I made several efforts to reach him. He would not return my calls to his office and if I phoned him at his apartment, he hung up. I even took the risk of calling a colleague of his to solicit his help. The colleague informed me that neither he nor anyone else in the office was close to Pieder. Every door was shut in my face. Finally all I could do was to pray for him and relinquish the problem to the Lord.

So far as I know, Pieder's was a life without repentance. His primary interest seemed to be power. Through her investment skills, Virginia had helped him make a great deal of money. The securities she advised him to buy were always in his name alone. Communication for him was wholly in the employ of his ulterior purposes. He could be impressively charming when he wanted to be; his gifts of intelligence and command made him the "ideal executive."

The weaker Virginia had become, the more aggressive he had become. Her defenselessness had only increased his cruelty. When she no longer interested him sexually, and when she was no longer useful to him financially after illness prevented her from holding a job, he was finished with her. Virginia never once heard him say, "I'm sorry."

When I pray for him I always see him sitting that evening in his living room with his face bowed into his hands. Was that maybe a tiny crack in his proud self-centeredness? I doubt if I'll ever know.

As Virginia recovered her physical strength, she continued to be in touch with me. One Saturday afternoon, sitting in the red, wing-backed chair in my study, Virginia said, "Love is a strange thing, isn't it? Do you know that somewhere inside my heart I still care for Pieder? He was cruel, imperious, hopelessly self-centered but there was a side of him, Joe, you never saw."

"Tell me about it."

"He could be completely charming when he wanted to be. He was probably the most well-educated man I ever knew. He read everything. There wasn't a subject you could raise on which he didn't have a really informed opinion. Time had a way of simply vanishing when we were lost in conversation on things we both knew a lot about—art for instance."

"It takes more to make a marriage than good conversation, Virginia."

"That's where it gets hard to describe." She paused, reflecting on what she was going to say. "I know this is tough for you to believe, Joe, but Pieder on very rare occasions could be as tender and playful as a kitten."

I waited. I sensed an emotional logjam about to move. She blurted, "Oh, Joe, if only I had been able to help him when he first turned the dark, cruel side of his face to me. That wasn't the real Pieder; I knew it wasn't!"

She wept, dried her tears, and went on. "You see, very early in our marriage I knew Pieder had an insatiable need for love and reassurance. It was a bottomless pit, and instead of trying to fill it or getting help to meet it, I only became frozen in fear."

There was nothing I could say. The enormity of all I knew held me silent.

"Fear killed my love for him. Everything I did was wrong. Again and again I saw his hunted eyes asking me to help him but by then he had begun to be violent with me."

"Are you saying, Virginia, now that your terror of Pieder has gone, your appreciation for him has come back?"

She nodded her agreement. Then she added firmly, "I know there was a time when love could have saved us, and I'm sorry, sorry, sorry. If only I could have reached him before he became so distant."

At the end of our visit I said, "Virginia, I want you to join me next Wednesday evening at a prayer group that meets at Calvary Church. There is a wonderful experience waiting for you."

Wednesday night when it came time for people to pray for one another, several of us gathered around Virginia. I laid my hands on her golden head. Others touched her gently on shoulders, feet, knees.

"Come, O Holy Spirit, and fill Virginia's heart. She belongs to You, she has given herself to You, she needs your forgiveness. Fill her, heal her, bless her. Let the flow of your love come upon her. Touch her with your pardon, your joy, your power. Illumine all the deep parts of her mind with the cleansing, sanctifying spirit of your perfect acceptance and peace. Help her to receive You afresh into her whole being. Give her a glorious new beginning this very night."

Virginia began to weep quietly. "O dear God, thank You! I've never felt such love in my life, wave upon wave of your joy. Thank You, thank You."

There was a pause, then she began to sing ever so quietly in a prayer language of purest joy. It was like the sweet song of a titmouse I heard in the mimosa tree outside my window as I wakened this morning. Virginia had returned to the Father's house.

To this day, Virginia knows that Jesus is hers and she is His. He was for her all along, as He was for Pieder all along. But some wall of tragic pride and preoccupation with power held even the Lord Christ out of Pieder's soul. Virginia chose to open herself to the boundless forgiveness and peace of a new life. Pieder did not.

That night as I drove up Park Avenue, leaving Calvary Church and a radiant Virginia behind me, I thought about Pieder all the way home. I too had seen that hunted look

in his eyes which Virginia had described. It was there that
first night at Norma's apartment when I saw him watching
me in conversation with Virginia. It was a wistfulness, an
outsider looking in. One day at New York Hospital I saw
it again when our paths crossed as we were visiting Virginia.
He is a driven man. There is a cleavage in his soul which
pushes him to justify himself by more and more worldly
success. *Dear God, I wish someone could help him.* I wonder where
he is now. Will pride and self-will prevent him from bending his knees forever?

It is the old, old tragic problem. Like Adam and Eve,
we would rather go it alone than submit our wills humbly
and obediently to the Lord and to His love. There is a
reptilian enmity at the center of our being, constantly
tempting us to leave the Father's kingdom, refusing His
rulership of our lives.

What a mighty thing is this tiny, vulnerable, changeable
reality we call the will. On its direction hangs our future.
On its faithfulness our characters are made. On its decisions
our salvation is shaped. The will is the core of our freedom.

Nowhere is the sublime humility of Jesus more lumi-
nously clear than when He comes to us imploring our devotion, begging for our obedience, with awesome patience,
entreating us to come home to the Father's house. What
a mystery is this: the Lord Christ, the beggar, beseeching
us to accept our health, knowing it is in the power of our
wills to reject or to follow Him, to remain stuck in our
old destructive patterns or to let Him lead us out to new
beginnings.

Chapter 5

The Loner

WHY IS IT so difficult to surrender ourselves to this healing, loving Lord? Could it be because, deep down, we fear that in so doing we will lose our own identity? That the new life He repeatedly offers us will be *His* life alone and no longer authentically ours?

I know there have been times in my life when I have shut out the Spirit of Joy Himself, preferring my own misery to some "external" influence, no matter how beneficent. I may be miserable, the subconscious argument must have gone, but at least I am myself, and not a rubber stamp of the Nazarene.

Gradually, however, I discovered a wonderful thing. I learned that the more unconditionally I gave myself to Christ, the more I became myself. Herein lies the surprise, something the secular world finds incomprehensible: the more we affirm the integrity of our own being, the more irresistible the desire becomes to give that being to the Lord. They are two sides of one coin, mutually supportive, each enhancing the other. The more committed we are to Him, the more completely we become the persons we truly are.

How can this be? What lies behind this depth of experience Christians have known ever since St. John wonderingly recorded the promise of Jesus: "I am come that they might have life, and that they might have it more abundantly"?

From my balcony here in the Tessin I can see the border of Italy, five miles away. My imagination carries me at once to the Umbrian hills and those geometric white dwellings piled one above the other, in the village of Assisi. If ever there was a man whose personhood became fulfilled through his commitment to the Lord, it was St. Francis.

Years ago I walked those hills in my bare feet. Everywhere I could sense the presence of the little troubadour. Sacred space is a mystery. The crypt in which the bones of the saint of Assisi are interred beneath the noble church, has a palpable holiness. I sat there a long time. It was the only place I visited in Italy where tourists fell into complete silence when they entered the room. What a little man he was. His coffin cannot be much more than four and one-half feet long.

The scenes of his life passed before my eyes as I sat in that crypt. His youthful mirth, his pleasure in companionship and games, his spontaneity and humor, and all the while his growing awareness of a subterranean stream of consciousness calling him to his holy destiny. That scene in which he runs after the beggar who had been refused alms at his father's shop was an early sign of what was to come.

Inevitably this maturing self-awareness led to tension between father and son. It became so intense that before the father left on one of his journeys to his beloved France—after which he had named his son—he locked the boy in his room. The father's ambitions for his son differed from the son's ambitions for himself.

All of us who attempt to force our children into a mold not their own live to rue the effort. The father of Francis certainly did, for the day came when there was an irrevocable break between the two.

Father and son face one another in the courtyard of the Bishop of Perugia. Francis is ready to declare himself unequivocally for who *he* is. Because of the control which fathers exercised over even adult offspring in that time and place, to become his own person required a total rupture. Francis disavows any interest in the estate his father has accumulated with a splendid future in mind for his son— even to the clothes on his back. He disrobes and before the shocked silence of the onlookers, lays every stitch at his father's feet, whereupon the bishop steps up to the little man of Assisi and embraces his nakedness in the voluminous folds of his cloak. Only now, having affirmed his independent selfhood, is Francis free to make the commitment of that self to God.

The rest is equally well known. The command of Christ to rebuild His church is first. Francis obeys with childlike literalness, repairing and remortaring a tiny edifice near his home, stone by stone, with his own hands. The vocation to poverty is there from the beginning. Only by refusing to allow any exterior claim on him can Francis retain his all-important freedom. There comes the slow, gradual gathering of those who join his vocation. Years later, recognition of his order is given by Rome. His fame spreads. Toward the end of his life of obedience and prayer, it happens: the awesome miracle of the stigmata, those bleeding scars on his hands, his side and his feet. St. Francis tries quickly to conceal this phenomenon but without success.

We should never forget that it was not the Christ of

miracles, nor the Christ of healing, nor the Christ of the Sermon on the Mount with whom Francis identified himself. It was the Christ of the Cross, the crucified Savior dying for the world, for you, for me, with whom Francis finally became one. But the disposition existed in Francis all along. Could there be any more vivid proof than that gesture, so well known, when the young Francis one day encounters a leper, alights from his horse and kisses the leper's lipless mouth?

Out of the 13th century there arises this man who responded unconditionally to the call of Christ to realize his full selfhood. To be a Christian is not just to have attitudes of kindness and compassion, nor to labor for justice and freedom, nor to embrace the human family with universal respect, valid and important though all of that is. To be a Christian is to know you are loved by One who has a name and by One who knows your name. To be a Christian is to be called: Name calling name.

It was his response to Christ which made Francis, Francis. He did not cease to be himself because he answered the calling of Jesus so unreservedly. On the contrary, before he could even give his answer, he had to claim his personhood. His father wanted to possess him, but the son knew—rare insight in feudal Europe—that no human being has the right to possess another. The father tried to understand his strange son, alternating between joyful exuberance and quiet solitude; when he failed, he resorted to coercion. But Francis knew that no one has the right to violate another's inwardness. My depths belong to my own domain. I have no right to invade another's inner being except by invitation any more than another has the right to invade mine. Each of us is and must remain unique.

When Francis gave himself to Christ, he had long lived in the depths of his own inward self. He had defined his objectives and made his own decisions. But it was only after that wholehearted self-giving that he blossomed as an individual person.

And what a blossoming it was! The whole of Western civilization was transformed at his touch. His compassion for the least of God's people, his joy in all creatures—beasts of the forest, wind, sun, moon—were the shining threads Francis wove into the tapestry of an evolving Christendom. Poverty, freely chosen, made him one with all who were oppressed by hunger and cold. Love, experienced in all cultures, became for Francis the style by which he made Jesus known to others. All of this made Francis no less a real person. It did not deprive him of his identity as a man, nor was he possessed by a foreign, inimical body. He was not split into two persons, one full of joy in all God's creation while the other schemed for his own advantage. Francis was whole. The calling of the Lord had integrated his character.

Nor did his vocation weaken his sense of who he was, nor from where he had come. It is significant that though he traveled far and wide, his roots were always in Perugia. Destiny took him to many impressive places of wealth and culture but he always came back to the little chapel where first he began to rebuild Christ's church. To the end, he remained the little troubadour of his native hills. He was Francis, transposed into an unimaginably beautiful key, which he himself perhaps never heard, so busy was he fulfilling his calling. But others heard it. The birds of the air heard it. Children saw it, and the dear, sainted Clare recognized it, founding her own order after the pattern of his. The new beginning Francis found in Christ was not the beginning of an alien and strange existence but of his own truest vocation.

Francis is a shining example from Christian history of

one whose personhood became confirmed, magnified, and illumined when he gave himself to the love of Christ. But in less dramatic ways I have observed the same reality in hundreds of contemporary men and women whose stories I have had reason to know over the years. I had a chance to watch this interdependence between being ourselves and being in Christ, this interweaving of faith and integrity, in a long friendship which began in World War II. It is quite different from the story of St. Francis. But it was the same Lord leading and blessing this man, enabling him to become more and more real with each renewing of his life in Christ.

Fred was a young fighter pilot on board a carrier on which I served as a chaplain during World War II. Unfortunately the time came when the medical officer of the ship and I agreed that the pressure of combat, the long months Fred had been on the ship, plus a history of intense introversion and withdrawal, had combined to create a severe anxiety neurosis in him. We thought it best to transfer him back to the states for medical treatment and possible discharge from service.

Fred vigorously resisted the suggestion when I raised the possibility with him. "I can't leave the best friends I have in the world, Padre. I'm no traitor."

We delayed a few weeks, but subsequent developments left us no choice. We shipped him home for hospital care.

A year after the war I had a Christmas card from Fred. "Big things are brewing," he wrote. "I may have some exciting news for you in a few months."

By this time Fred was living in Hanover, New Hampshire, where he had obtained a teaching fellowship while completing work for his Ph.D. in English at Dartmouth College. Correspondence soon revealed happy expectations of marriage.

His fiancée was from Pittsburgh. They had met in Washington at the end of the war while Fred was under treatment at the Veterans Hospital, and she was working for the State Department. He couldn't have been more lyrical in describing Isobel to me. Could I come to do the service in the garden of her home?

Isobel was beautiful, alive, trim-figured, with large brown eyes and a smile which made the edges of her mouth tip upward in an innocence as real as it was transparent. The only flaw in this creation of loveliness was a faint birthmark which splotched the right side of her face from her upper cheekbone to the hairline. But it could hardly be called a defect, adding as it did a certain distinction to her finely drawn features.

Fred was even taller than I remembered him, still carrying himself as though he were on a ship tilting to starboard. His hair was carrot red, growing from the front in a cowlick. Maybe it was that red hair which made his eyes so penetratingly blue. His nose was larger than life. He laughed but rarely, though his smile was quick and easy to come by. An excellent position had been offered Fred at the recommendation of the chairman of his department at Dartmouth. The promise of his career was outstanding due to the original quality of his mind and to a prodigious capacity for hard work. Fred's parents were unreservedly happy about everything, particularly about Isobel. The years after discharge from the Navy had not been easy. Now, however, that tunnel seemed to be passed.

Each wedding is a little different from every other one. There is a mystery in marriage which never fails to touch me. And so it was that day in a garden filled with early June flowers. We stood under an ancient oak tree whose generous branches reached out to shade all 40 or 50 of us. It was a beautiful, poignant moment of new beginning.

Everyone present knew the patience, the hope, the dogged faith in God which had made this day possible.

A friendship of priceless worth began among the three of us as we found ourselves living but 12 miles from one another shortly thereafter.

About a year after the wedding, Fred began to complain of constant fatigue. His weight loss was not evident to most people because he had never been heavy, and his long ruddy face was always creased with lines. But I noticed it and commented on it to Isobel one evening while Fred was out of the room. I could see a gathering fear in her eyes. I took a pad and pencil from my pocket and wrote on it the name of a doctor at the university hospital who had an outstanding reputation.

"Get Fred to make an appointment with him soon," I told her. "It's doubtless nothing serious, but let's check it out."

About a fortnight later Isobel called me: "Joe, it's cancer of the lymph glands—lymphoma."

"I'll be there this afternoon, Isobel."

The two of them were waiting for me in the apartment when I arrived. It was a hot, sticky day, one of those sudden bursts of heat we sometimes get in early June. Fred was in his shirt sleeves, lying on the sofa, his face strangely serene.

After Isobel had provided iced tea, I said, "What's the treatment they're proposing?"

"Radiation," Isobel replied. This was before the development of chemotherapy, and radiation was then our greatest weapon in cancer treatment.

"You both know," I said, "how strongly I believe in the power of prayer through the Spirit to affect our bodies."

They both nodded eagerly. Fred moved to a straight-backed chair and I laid my hands on his head, invoking

the healing power of Christ as a divine flow of renewing
strength and energy, praying that God would touch the
secret source of life within Fred's body, mind, and soul.
Afterwards Fred turned to me and with quiet composure
said, "Joe, I know how serious all this is. Ever since that
time on the carrier when I received the Lord Christ into
my heart, I've been trying to give myself more totally to
him. Will you help me to do it now?"

It caught me off guard. "Why, Fred, yes, to be sure," I
fumbled. "Is there anything special you want to say to God,"
I added, "before we pray?"

"No, Joe, I've been trying to be real with the Lord every
night for a long time now. He knows all about me. I want
to make it complete now."

I was thunderstruck. Where had I been? This close friend
had been ready for a new beginning, a new depth of commitment to Christ, and I had been unaware of it.

So we continued to pray, only this time it was Fred who
spoke: "Lord, I am all yours. I put myself and anything
that happens into Your hands. From this moment for eternity, I am Yours. I promise to trust You, Lord Jesus, no
matter what."

Naturally all this was accompanied by deep emotion
among us; each of the three of us sensed that regardless
of his physical appearance, the essential life in Fred had
been marvelously restored, integrated, renewed. Soon afterwards I left for Rhode Island and my summer rest.

During my vacation I thought and prayed about Fred
and Isobel many times. What a remarkable thing I had seen
that day before my departure. Here was a man whose inte-
rior anxieties were once so severe he could barely bring
himself to speak with a stranger. The captain of his squad-
ron referred to him as a "loner." When we had divine services on board ship he always sat in the last row, as incon-

spicuous as possible, and when he took the chalice at the kneeling rail his hands always shook. The other pilots said he was a superb fighter once he had his hands on the controls of his plane; but they also commented that they had never seen a pilot sweat so much when flying. And now a few short years later the same man facing a terminal illness was confessing to God that he was ready to trust Him "no matter what."

What was it that had brought the conflicting forces in Fred to a unified center? How had it happened that Fred's privacy had changed from an inner preserve of defensiveness and fear to a pool of deep waters he could share with others? How had he come by that inner harmony? There could be only one conclusion: Fred had become an integrated and genuine being as and to the degree that he surrendered that being to the Lord.

When I saw them again after vacation I could see what a toll the disease had taken, not only on Fred but on Isobel too. Her face was drawn and tight, and I began to pick up a quality of anger in her voice.

Fred was restless on the sofa, and Isobel suggested he might be more comfortable in bed. After she returned from getting Fred settled, I asked, "Isobel, what are you so angry about?"

"Joe, I hope you won't think it's silly of me or unwise or wrong, but I know Fred is dying and he knows it, and I want more than anything in the world to have his child."

"Why, Isobel, of course I understand that. What's the problem?"

"Fred won't cooperate," Isobel said, tears suddenly beginning to overcome her tight control.

"Why not?"

"He says it's not fair to leave me with such a responsibility—one he can't share."

"But surely you can see what he means."

"Oh," blazed Isobel, dark eyes flashing, "you're just like Fred. I might have known you would take his side. We've been fighting about this for the past two weeks until we can barely talk civilly to one another."

I decided we needed time for some perspective, so I said nothing, but dug in my pocket for my pipe, carefully filled it, slowly lit it, and puffed on it awhile.

"Listen to me, Honey," I began. "You know better than I do that Fred needs your love these days, not your anger and your rejection."

It was the worst thing I could have said. The fire was blazing hot again.

"What about me? I'm going to be left behind without him! Doesn't anyone think about my feelings?"

"I am thinking about your feelings, Isobel, and so is Fred. He knows you are still young and beautiful. You've got your whole life before you. You should be free to go on with it as opportunity provides and not be held back with the responsibility of a child."

"Oh, you men! You're all alike. Don't you see I don't look at it that way at all? I love Fred. I adore him. I'll never love anyone else the way I love him. That's the way it is and that's the way I am, and I want a part of him left with me," suddenly heading for the bathroom door, adding, "after he's gone."

She shut the door and all I could hear was the faucet running full tilt. When she came back, I said quickly, "Isobel, forgive me. Please forgive my stupid, obtuse head. I've been praying about this while you were out of the room, and that's what I should have done in the first place. Of course you are right. That's the way love is. It's love that wants the child and it's Fred's concern for you that doesn't want the child, but I now know it's a greater love to want it. I'll talk to Fred. Give us some time. We'll work it out."

She came over to my chair and kissed me.

At first, Fred resisted my pleas. He stood squarely against me as he had with Isobel. Help came from an unexpected quarter as it often does in God's providence. Fred's father came for a weekend visit in early October.

"Fred, can't you see I want your child, my grandchild, as much as Isobel does? We'll take care of Isobel. You don't need to worry about that, and Isobel is a pretty capable gal, too, don't you forget."

That did it. Fred's resistance had no more ground to stand on. Around Christmas on one of my visits to them I took Fred a little book, *Healing Prayer,* by William Portsmouth. Prayer had become as natural as breathing for the three of us. That day we prayed with much earnestness that Isobel might become pregnant. Fred was now as eager for it as previously he had been against it.

To see them together was unforgettable. When they conversed, their eyes constantly met and danced in each other's love. Fred was still teaching, though on a reduced schedule. They cherished every hour together. They could hardly be in the same room without some part of their bodies touching—hands, feet, thighs, shoulders. It was their transparent faith in God which allowed them to be so open and human with one another.

A few weeks after Christmas, Isobel told Fred she thought it had happened. In early February Fred called me and said, "Well, Joe, this was one prayer that was answered the way we wanted it to be. Isobel is pregnant! The baby's due in September."

After that Fred wanted to live only to see his child. However he was hospitalized in March. There was an operation, but the surgeon did nothing because of the massive spread of the disease. Fred died on April 20, "the cruelest of months."

At the funeral, the church was full of their friends. We

held it in Pittsburgh where Isobel had decided to live. He was buried in her family plot.

During the service I said a few brief things. Of course, my text was, "If God be for us, who can be against us?" I did not try to minimize the tragedy which had occurred. I said we had to learn to live in a world of infinite possibility where death and disease could happen to any of us at any time. Sometimes through prayer I had seen miraculous things happen in overcoming disease, and sometimes not. This was one of those times when the answer in this world was "no," and I prayed that we would be given the faith to believe that though the answer had been "no" to us, it was not a "no" for Fred.

Then I told of an experience Fred and I had during the war. It was my practice when combat conditions permitted it, to offer the sacrament of holy communion early every morning in the library of the ship. Fred always came.

One morning he was the only one present. After he had received the wine from the chalice, I continued with the usual prayers of intercession and thanksgiving. When I turned to give the blessing, Fred was still kneeling there at the altar rail, eyes glistening, face radiating a joy you couldn't miss. He saw my puzzled expression. "Padre, the love of the Lord Jesus Christ has just come into my heart. Such love it is! Such love it is!"

And this from a man who'd had a dreadfully hard time accepting any love at all. I laid my hands upon him and declared that this was the true beginning of a new and indestructible life in Christ.

I concluded my remarks at the funeral by saying, "Fred now knows in a way we cannot yet know, that because God is for him not even death can be against him. I believe Fred's steady victory over anxiety, his growing freedom to love and be loved, his increasing faith in Christ's love in spite of a life-threatening disease, all began that day in that steel-walled room on board that ship. His commitment to Christ became a commitment to himself, and out of that beginning the pearl of a person we know as Fred emerged."

Their baby was born on September 19 and it was a boy! Another new beginning. That was a very special baptismal service. I put water on that child and named him Frederick Ames after his father. And to think he will be 28 years old on his next birthday.

I have told Fred's story at some length because the humanity of each of us was so greatly deepened as together we deepened our commitment to the Lord. Fred's fear of betraying his co-pilots if he had to return to the states, Isobel's determination to have Fred's child, the funeral service, the baptismal occasion with Isobel standing alone a few steps ahead of the four grandparents, proudly lifting little Frederick into my arms—all belong to the vocabulary of what makes us fully human.

But this humanity was warmed and kindled by the breath of the Holy Spirit. Through intimacy with God we grew closer to each other than we could ever have been otherwise. We were more real and open to one another because we first dared to be real and open with Him. Selfhood and self-surrender—they are like the two halves of a single cell which came together at the beginning of our physical life, two partial entities which had to merge before birth and growth were possible.

Chapter 6

Born Again . . . and Again

BECAUSE, OF COURSE, the experiences that I am calling "new beginnings," are what many Christian traditions know as "new birth." New beginnings, new birth: both phrases are attempts to describe what happens to us when we accept the love of Christ which is always on our side. Christ's love, St. John tells us, is a light shining through the boundless network of sin which mankind has woven over the centuries of misused freedom. In spite of the fearful opacity of that network, the light, in the words of the fourth Gospel, shines on and the darkness "comprehended it not."

New birth occurs when a person comes face to face with his own participation in that network of resistance and rebellion. Before his horrified inner gaze he sees the damage he has inflicted, the hurt he has caused, the sins he has committed, and when the season of readiness has ripened within his soul, he begs for the love of God to take over his life, and to accomplish the change he knows he is powerless to do alone. When the gift of that Christly love is received, we say he has been converted, reborn, as St. John tells us, "not of blood, nor of the will of the flesh, nor of the will of man, but of God."

The time has come in Christendom for this mighty and seminal experience of regeneration to be reclaimed for all the body of believers. We owe an incalculable debt to those evangelical Christians who have preserved the pivotal importance of this rebirth; the sheer consistency of their witness over many centuries should command the grateful respect of all of us.

However, let us not forget that the new birth experience is available to many different traditions of Christianity. It is imperative that we reverence the diversity of these traditions without disparaging them if they do not happen to conform to our own. The Spirit "blows where it wills" as Jesus reminds Nicodemus when describing the necessity of being born again.

I have been present at services—I have occasionally officiated at them—in which people were invited to come forward to an altar in token of their intention to accept Christ from that moment forward as their personal Lord and Savior. I have known countless people who have had their lives wholly refashioned by such a one-time decision.

Yet as I look back over my own personal experience of conversion, I realize that it has been a continuous process with me—not one experience of rebirth but many. It never ceases. I am dumbfounded at the Lord's patience with me. It seems He knows my need is limitless so He never fails to provide me with a new dimension of His presence.

The first parish I ever served was in 1940 in Monroe, Wisconsin. I was unmarried and lived with two saints in their 60s. They were both teachers: one taught kindergarten, the other fifth grade. The affection and joy among us was a gift we cherished.

Aunt Ethel had a small goiter on her neck. One evening just before I went to my room for the night, she asked me to pray about it. "I believe the Lord could heal this thing, don't you?"

Except in the New Testament I had never heard of "the laying on of hands," but instinctively I did so as Aunt Ethel sat before me. I wince now as I recall the scene in her living room: I a mere lad with almost no understanding of the depths of life and she a bright-eyed soul well along in years with an absolute trust in the love of Jesus, having molded the lives of hundreds of young children. With my hands on her white head, all I could think to pray was, "Lord Jesus, this is an easy one for You. Everything is possible for You. Heal Aunt Ethel's goiter, I pray, and kindly accept our thanks."

That's all there was to it, but the next morning Aunt Ethel met me as I came down the stairs for breakfast. "Take a look," she said.

The goiter was gone.

I grasped the newel post and said, "Aunt Ethel you could knock me over with a feather." I was so astonished that I even forgot to praise God. Aunt Ethel's friend and housemate, Grace Byers, did it for us at the breakfast table.

It was a life-forming experience, a time of rebirth in Christ for me. It shaped much of what was to come in the following decades.

Yet it was not my first rebirth, nor my last. The first one I remember occurred when I was 14 years old and home for vacation from boarding school—St. Paul's in Baltimore, now a day school. My life at St. Paul's had been increasingly filled with a mystic sense of the divine presence. Mrs. Kinsolving, the rector's wife, was an Anglo-Catholic who somehow sensed a wistful, poignant yearning of the soul in me. She had befriended me and given me things to read. Much of it was wholly beyond me. But when we boys in the school choir sang "Let all mortal flesh keep silence and with fear and trembling stand" before the sacrament was offered us by the sainted Dr. Kinsolving, I very often did tremble. I remember once after taking the sacrament I fainted, stupid and embarrassed afterwards, but not without the certainty that something quite real had brushed my soul.

Now, home in Washington, D.C., for Christmas, I walked alone up Massachusetts Avenue from our home on Q Street to the Washington Cathedral for the Christmas Eve service. Dean Stokes, very tall and wearing pince-nez glasses, looked sternly at the congregation. As I recall, he said something to the effect that since Christmas was the celebration of the birth of our Lord, there was no more wonderful way in which we could honor Him than to allow Him to be born in us that day.

Consequently, as we came to the altar rail and knelt to receive the sacrament, he asked each of us a question before offering us the chalice:

"Will you receive Christ as your Lord and Savior?"

To which I replied with a young heart so ardent and full I thought I would burst, "I will." Then he gave me the cup saying, "This is the blood of Christ shed for you. Drink this and be thankful."

I never remember returning to my seat, but I knew beyond all doubt that night that the Lord Jesus and I had met. He was for *me,* not only for the whole world but for me. I needed to know that at 14. He would be henceforth my Lord and Savior, my friend and companion, my stay and guide.

I remember later trying to tell my family something of all this. They didn't understand. Indeed, the phrase "religious fanatic" was used, not in malice nor with any intention of rejection, simply with concern that I was getting in over my head. I didn't talk about this part of my life again at home for a long time.

The reality of that first experience of the living Spirit of Christ has never left me. I realize now in my 60s that it was the foundation stone on which everything else was built. I suppose that is one reason why each year's confirmation class in my present church in Rye, New York, is so important to me. I yearn for "my" young people to have an experience as real and important for them as my early experience was for me.

For years therefore I have been teaching the eighth grade confirmation class about the Christian faith in a way which urges them to anticipate an experience of the Lord's living presence. During the week before Pentecost Sunday, when for the first time our young people make their public commitment to Jesus Christ, I meet with them individually in an all-night vigil of prayer.

We begin the evening about 9 P.M. with some general sharing, singing, and refreshments. The adults who assist me are as committed as I to the values we are seeking, and their prayers are crucial to the effectiveness of the night. The young people are kept under a discipline of quietness and prayer. As I well know, so much depends on that mysterious reality called readiness. If the young people are ready for a genuine breakthrough of the Spirit, an unforgettable encounter happens.

All through the night they come into the chapel to be alone with me, one by one. The class usually includes about 40 young people, so naturally it is dawn or a little later when we finish. As each young person is escorted into the chapel by one of the chaperones, I watch with real emotion as she or he approaches. Many of them I have known since birth and baptized not a few when they were infants.

The chapel is lit only by the two candles on the altar. Chairs are situated at either end of the holy table, face to face. We sit down and I say something personal to each young person about our friendship or the family background. Sometimes I'm aware that there is a crisis in the family's life, and if appropriate I gently raise the issue. I ask if there is any problem of faith or any other question the young person wishes to raise with me, any burden he or she would like to share.

It is an exceedingly special time. I truly love every one of them. My whole being thirsts for them to begin their lives rooted in Christ. There the girl or boy sits before me. The gleaming cross on the altar, symbol of the Savior's love, casts its reflection over us. Our voices are low. We are wrapped in the sublime mystery of holiness. The eyes of the young person before me glow with eager expectation, although as the night plods on toward a new day, many are roused from sleep in order to come in to the chapel.

This past year one young man sat down in the chair opposite me, eyes dancing, his whole body alive. He reached his hands into the air as far as he could stretch them: "Man, this place is crawling with the Holy Spirit!"

After we have talked, naturally in some cases longer than others, I ask each young person either to kneel or remain seated in the chair, whichever seems most natural; then I stand behind him and lay hands on him to invoke the blessing of the Holy Spirit.

At the conclusion of the prayer for the Lord's holy nearness, I ask each one the most important question possible: Is he or she now ready to make a life commitment to Jesus? When the answer is yes, I ask, "Who is your Lord and Savior?"

"Jesus Christ is my Lord and Savior."

"Do you trust Him?"

"I do."

We then share a prayer of thanksgiving, and I walk with the young person down the aisle of the chapel. Not infrequently there have been tears. We part with an embrace.

My mind often dwells on these hundreds of young people in their hour of rebirth in Christ, and I am led to pray that there will be as many such new beginnings in their lives as there is need of them. Because the need will come, again and again.

During the war as a chaplain in the Aleutians, I began to lose the sense of God's closeness. The boredom, the loneliness, the 21-hour nights of the far-northern winter afflicted us all. I spent countless hours listening to the frustrations of men in that tundra-covered, treeless countryside. The ceaseless wind was like a menace of malignant power—"williwaws," we called it.

It began to get to me. In the mornings I could barely speak to anyone. I felt myself being sucked into a black hole from which there was no escape. I prayed and prayed but nothing happened: "Words, words, nothing but words." Days became so many hours to get through.

I now think the Lord was trying to reach me all the time, but I was wallowing so much in my own misery that He couldn't get through my self-pity. Consequently He sent Bobby Moore into my life. He was assigned to help me with several of my duties including the care of the library. There was a quality of confidence, warmth and humor in the man which was like an oasis to me in a desert time.

After our first time of prayer together, I knew he was more the minister to me than I was to him. God had sent him to me to point the way to the new beginning I was too self-absorbed to find. Bob's prayers were of the simplest character, never more than a phrase or two, but in the silence which followed, there was an unforgettable presence of the

Lord. Never before nor since have I felt so keenly the power of the words, "For where two or three are gathered together in my name, there am I in the midst of them."

It taught me something I have never forgotten. We are not intended to walk the path of faith alone. Today I find myself urging people whose lives seem to have reached a dead end to get into prayer fellowship, to find a prayer partner. Bobby Moore was God's way of telling me that the Lord is for us even in our depressions if we will but look around and discover the messenger He has sent.

Nor can I forget how the Spirit came to me, later in the war, in those early morning celebrations of holy communion on board an aircraft carrier of which I have already written in telling the story of Fred and Isobel. Again and again the Lord was in that tiny, steel-clad room blessing me, giving me new life, providing the strength to do what I could never have done otherwise during those days.

In my mature ministry I shall always remember what Agnes Sanford and Lydia Maxam did for me in an upper room at Lasell House in Whitinsville, Massachusetts. It was 20 years ago, but it seems like yesterday. Again I was feeling as though God had departed from my ministry. I was confused, overtired, wearied by a series of life's injustices to me personally, desperately in need of yet another new beginning. And they laid their hands upon me. Agnes voiced the prayer of forgiveness for my sin of unforgiveness, and Lydia called on me to relinquish everything to the Lord. They became the channel of His healing and I felt the love of Christ overwhelming me again. I wept and thanked Him in a tongue of praise I had never known before, and once again I knew He was for me, not only the world and all people, but me! Wonder of wonders. I could witness to His love again.

My experience of conversion has been, then, one glowing birth following another, each one chastening and humbling me to deeper levels of worship and praise than before, each coming as a response to great need. Each is equally valid if the fruit of the life reborn in Christ yields its blessed harvest of "love, joy, peace, longsuffering, gentleness, goodness, faith, meekness, and temperance."

However, although in my own life such new beginnings have been frequent, each of us can recall people whose walk in Christ was so steadfast that no crisis of conversion ever appears to have occurred. Had they dredged up from their past some long-forgiven sin or separation in order to "qualify" for rebirth, it would have seemed almost unnatural, out of character, abortive. I have wondered if such people came into their rebirth in the Spirit at such an early age—perhaps soon after physical birth itself—that they could never consciously recapture the event.

There is such a person in my life—one who taught me more about the love of Christ than anyone I have ever known. She was "Aunt Mary" to me. Wherever there was need in our village of Mercersburg, Pennsylvania, she was there. If it was sickness, she was at the bedside. If it was grief, she was quietly present. If it was calamity, an accident, a family deserted, she was the first on the scene with material assistance.

I can see her face now, patrician nose, pince-nez glasses, white hair parted in the middle and bound in a bun in the back. I suppose she wore other colors, but I always think of her in white with lace collar and ankle-length skirt. She had two sisters, in a family of five, who were dwarfs. The care of those sisters fell on her from their middle life to their deaths. They were easily irritated and given to pettiness, but in all the hours I spent in Aunt Mary's house by day and night, I never heard her speak a cross word in rebuke. Instead, it was always a tinkling soft laughter by which she indulged her charges and jollied them out of their woeful moods.

When I slept at her house, my room was next to hers. I took it to be the most natural thing in the world that she spent what seemed to my youthful mind a very long time every night reading the Bible. She knew hundreds of texts by memory as she also knew endless stanzas of hymns which she hummed to herself as she went about her daily chores. Her church was as important a part of her life as her home. Her forebears had founded it, long before the present building, when the village was only an outpost in Indian territory.

Aunt Mary couldn't remember a time when her life wasn't in the blessed care of Jesus. I heard her say so to my mother many times. It was as though her very first new beginning in God—older than memory—kept its freshness and wonder through more than 80 years, a fountain of supernatural joy in her I never knew to fail.

The last time I saw her was in a nursing home run by the United Brethren. The facility was small, not accommodating more than 50 residents, and for that reason, among others, it was a very human place. Aunt Mary's mind had deteriorated, but her spirit was as gracious and Christlike as ever. I've often counseled people, "You'd better give attention to your spiritual growth, because if your body outlives your mind, the only thing left is your character." Aunt Mary's character was unchanged to the end. The only book she had by her bed was her Bible, and the nurse told me that before the light was put out each night Aunt Mary had to read a few verses. I'd like to think she knew who I was on that last visit. All I know is that her smile and her kiss were just the same, the Christ-light in her as bright as ever.

At the opposite end of the pole from dear Christian souls like Aunt Mary is the experience of a young man who lived nearly 1,600 years ago. In a walled garden in Milan, Italy, in 387, a conversion took place which shaped the entire future of Christendom. The mother of this man had prayed for his commitment to Christ from his birth, but unlike Aunt Mary he resisted violently for 33 years. When he was 19, he did feel a strong tidal wave of supernatural power drawing him to Christ, but he was not yet ready and for 14 more years he refused to be drawn into the ocean of that mighty and mysterious love.

His was a passionate, gifted nature. Everything was felt with more than usual intensity. The play of the senses was an endless ecstasy to him. He wrote of himself as a young man, "My one delight was to love and to be loved. But in this I could not distinguish the white light of love from the fog of lust. Both love and lust boiled within me and swept my youthful immaturity over the precipice of evil desires to leave me half drowned in a whirlpool of abominable sins. I came to Carthage where a cauldron of illicit loves leapt and boiled about me. I was not yet in love, but I was in love with love . . . within I was hungry for the want of that spiritual food which is Thyself, my God, yet I did not hunger for it. I had no desire whatever for incorruptible food, not because I had it in abundance, but the emptier I was, the more I hated the thought of it."

In this state of lustful pursuit, driving himself to ever more intense forms of sexual fulfillment, insatiable in his demands for love and ego affirmation, the man's health broke again and again. For 14 years he vacillated between doubt and belief, between hope and despair. For well over a decade he dallied with a sect of his time called Manicheism. This was a philosophical position about God and nature which took a posture of arrogant superiority toward all religions, scorning especially Christianity's claim that Jesus was the Word made flesh. The literature of the Manichean philosophers was thought to be vastly above the Bible in its purity of language and literary imagery.

During this early time of his life, a son was born to him. The mother of the child then went out of his life and left the boy in his care. Speaking of his awe and devotion for this child, the father later wrote, "I had the experience of many remarkable qualities in him. His great intelligence filled one with a kind of awe, and who but You could be the maker of things so wonderful? But You took him early from this earth, and I think of him utterly without anxiety, for there is nothing in his boyhood—or anywhere in him— to cause me fear."

But though the loss of his son affected him profoundly, there continued to be much procrastination, delay, resistance, regression into old habits and old pleasures which had long enslaved him. When he met Faustus, the leader of the Manicheans, he was abysmally disappointed. It became an occasion for looking again toward the faith to which his mother clung so faithfully, humbly, unswervingly.

For all of his literary sophistication, the authority of the Bible began to grip him with ever greater potency. It was an authority which went beyond a moral imperative, though the truth of its teachings was not lost upon his intelligence, nor was it an authority imposed by a saintly mother. It was an authority which simply stepped from the pages of Holy Writ and said, "Thus saith the Lord." It was not a question of rhetorical debate regarding truth at which this brilliant man excelled. It was rather a perception of the sphere of holiness to which the only possible response was obedience or disobedience.

Of course I have been describing Augustine, the great

teacher, bishop and saint of Christendom. We know all this about him because with consummate skill he has told us of his struggles in a book called *Confessions*.

Even after he began to recognize the authority of Scripture, something held him back from the final break with the past, the radical new beginning which it demanded. More years were to pass while he discarded the Bible, came back to it, fled its claims and went back to it again. At long last the crisis was reached. The towering intellect and passionate nature of Augustine had brought him at last to the moment of decision. Let us hear his own words as he addresses God:

. . . I wanted to follow you! My soul hung back. It would not follow, yet found no excuse for not following. All its arguments had already been used and rejected. There remained only trembling silence. In the midst of this great tumult . . . I turned to Alypius, a treasured friend, wild in look, crying out "What is wrong with us? The unlearned arise and take heaven by force, and here are we with all our learning stuck fast in flesh and blood!" These words and more of the same I uttered, then the violence of my feeling tore me from Alypius.

There was a garden attached to our house, of which we had the use . . . To this garden the storm in my breast somehow brought me . . . There I was, going mad on my way to sanity, dying on my way to life . . . I was frantic . . . for not going over to your law and your covenant, O my God, where all my bones cried out I should be . . . I had only to will to go— but to will powerfully and wholly, not to turn and twist a will half wounded this way and that with the part that would rise struggling against the part that would keep to the earth.

Why this monstrousness? And what is the root of it? The mind gives the body an order, and is obeyed at once: the mind gives itself an order and is resisted. The trouble is it does not totally avail; therefore it does not totally command. It commands in so far as it wills and it disobeys the command in so far as it does not will.

I kept saying to myself "Let it be now! Let it be now!" I almost made it but not quite. I tried again and I was almost there and now I could all but touch it and hold it. Yet I was not there. I shrank from dying unto death and living unto life . . . The nearer the point of time came in which I was to become different, the more it struck me with horror.

These trifles, all trifles, my one-time mistresses—plucking at my garments of flesh and murmuring softly, "Are you going to send us away. From this moment shall this or that not be allowed to you?" The strong force of habit said to me, "Do you think you can live without them?"

When my searching scrutiny had drawn up all my vileness from the secret depth of my soul, and heaped it in my heart's sight, a mighty storm arose in me, bringing a mighty rain of tears. I arose and flung myself under a fig tree and no longer tried to check my tears.

I continued my miserable complaining, how long shall I go on saying, tomorrow and again tomorrow? Why not now?

. . . And suddenly I heard a voice from some nearby house— it was sort of sing song repeated again and again, "Take and read. Take and read." I ceased weeping and began to search my mind as to whether children were accustomed to chant those words in any kind of game and I could not remember that I had ever heard such a thing. Damming back the flood of tears I arose, interpreting the incident as a Divine Command to open my book of scriptures and read the passage at which I should open.

So I moved to the place where Alypius was sitting, for I had put down the Apostle's book there. I snatched it up, opened it, and in silence read the passage on which my eyes first fell, "Not in rioting and drunkenness, not in chambering and impurities, not in contention and envy, but put ye on the Lord Jesus Christ and make not provision for the flesh in its concupiscences" (Romans 13;13–14). I had no wish to read further or a need to do so. For in that instant, with the very ending of the sentence, it was as though a light of utter confidence shone in all my heart, and all the darkness of uncertainty vanished away . . . Then leaving my finger in the place, I closed the book and in complete calm told the whole thing to Alypius.

Next he hastened to share the news with his mother, Monica, whose joy knew no bounds. In confirmation of his new birth he was baptized and received into the body of Christ in Milan. "I wept at the beauty of your hymns and canticles, and was powerfully moved at the sweet sound of your church's singing. Those sounds flowed into my ears, and the truth streamed into my heart, so that my feeling of devotion overflowed, and the tears ran from my eyes, and I was happy in them."

At the age of 33 Augustine had been born again, more painfully, more slowly, more violently than is the experience of many of us, but taking at last that all-determining step of trust and acceptance with which the great journey begins.

Chapter 7

When the Road Is Long:
The Story of Annie West

If NEW BIRTH is like a single step—whether taken once and for all or repeated many times—the life in Christ into which we are born can be likened to a daily walk. *In Christ*—those are the crucial words. From henceforth our life journey is to be spent in the company of the One we have decided to believe.

Naturally, in the course of any journey we begin to know the person who travels with us. With time and shared experience, this knowledge deepens. From that Christmas evensong service in Washington to this hour on Lago Maggiore, mine has been a long, long journey with the Lord. He knows me wholly. I know Him still but partially. Like that railing on the Eiffel Tower I grab ahold of Him when I feel myself falling. Every time I do, I discover He is already holding on to me. He never lets me go. I hold fast when it suits my purpose. He sacrifices Himself completely for me. I give Him what is convenient and comfortable. He becomes poor and humble for my sake. I often prefer to hold all the power in my own hands.

Yet, time, which is another word for grace, ticks on while Jesus and I labor with one another. As the years go on, deeper and deeper levels in our relationship are forged until now I should be lying if I did not say it is a holy intimacy. Let it be clear: it is obviously not a relation of equals. He is the Lord! Nor is it a relationship which may be likened to any other. I have often tried to do so. I cherished beyond measure the stage in life when my children were young. No satisfaction or joy is quite like it. Yet, Father-child does not really describe His dealings with me.

Nor can I liken my intimacy with Christ to my relations with my dearest friends or even my spouse. It is a relationship to that distinct, recognizable, consistent, inimitable, unique gospel-figure I would know anywhere, in broad daylight or in the darkest of nights. I know His voice. I am familiar with His step. His wrath is not foreign to my ears nor are His judgments lacking in my experience. I know what makes Him weep, and I have heard His deep warming, contagious laughter. I know His healing hands. Over and over I have heard Him say to me, "Thy sins are forgiven thee; rise up and begin again."

Clearly my experience is typical. There is nothing unique about it. There is a similarity between it and the experience of Christians everywhere, past and present. The quality, the timing, the degree, the specifics vary infinitely. But the essential relation is the same for all of us. And like all relations it requires attention, time and trust to preserve it.

There is someone in whose experience of Christ I have seen this trust increasingly at work. Her heart has become more fixed in Christ with each new birth in Him, but the anguish of beginning again has been extreme, and the demands of perseverance have been enormous.

We have known each other for almost 30 years. When we meet it is as though we had parted from one another yesterday, although our get-togethers now are rare. But when first we knew each other we saw one another almost every day. She lived two houses from mine.

Her feet are not her own to command as are mine, nor are her hands, nor her tongue. Her handicap since birth from the affliction of cerebral palsy is all-encompassing. Yet the remarkable thing is that as soon as you meet her you forget her physical limits.

Her name is Annie. I am one of the few people she will permit to call her Annie, so it is that name I shall use in telling her story.

When I first knew her, she had finished her college work at Drew University. She naturally required a wheelchair which her ingenious and devoted father had improved in several ways, including a motor. He was a professor of chemistry and could do almost anything with his hands; so Annie's chair was a marvel of efficiency.

Various people had discouraged the family from urging Annie on with her education. Everyone recognized the presence of a highly gifted intelligence, but all things considered, why should the family assume the burden of more schooling? What future was there for Annie? That, however, was never the attitude of her parents. They agreed that if Annie wanted an education, she would have it no matter how long it took or at what sacrifice.

When college was finally completed, though, there was, predictably, no job for Annie. It was impossible for her to live alone. In a college setting, volunteers had always been found to help with the routines most of us take for granted: getting up, dressing, toileting, getting to meals, positioning a straw for liquids, cutting solid food into edible bites. But to go into the working world and find such assistance seemed out of the question. It was beyond her family's means to hire such a helper so home she had to come.

We had a nursery school at our church at the time, headed by a genius of a person, more gifted in helping three- and four-year-olds recognize themselves as persons than anyone I have ever known. Her name was Mimi. I told Mimi about my concerns for Annie one day and she asked, "Why doesn't she join our staff?"

"Mimi, I don't understand. What could Annie do for us?"

"She majored in psychology, didn't she?"

"Well, yes, but how would you use that here?"

"I'd have her do studies of children I'm concerned about. You say she uses a typewriter. She could type her observations, then she and I could arrange a private conference with the parents to talk over Annie's analysis. And besides, think what a learning experience it would be for the children to relate to Annie on an everyday basis."

So it was arranged. We found a little money—a pittance, really—to pay Annie enough to preserve some dignity, and morning after morning I would see her come down the ramp at her house with either parent's help. Then she was off on her own in her motorized chair, going down the street to the church with her notebook and pad tucked in the pocket at the side, her stronger left hand clutching the controls which let her stop at the red lights and make the necessary turns.

If I knew what a badge of courage was or where I could find one, I would have put it on Annie's "chariot." Anyone looking at that eager, small face of hers, the straight hair cut in bangs, those wide expressive blue eyes, pushing toward her labor of love every day, would be bound to say, "And I think I've got problems." This was Annie's way of life for two or three years.

My own children were in the nursery school. Tim, our

middle son, was one of Annie's "special" children. She described an insecurity in our dear Tim at the age of four which helped us to deal with him in a more constructive and sensitive way than we had done previously. There were countless other families she helped. Her perceptions were keen, accurate, expressed with great compassion.

One day, at about 5 P.M. as I was returning to my house from the church, I felt a compelling, irresistible, mandatory call to go to see Annie. I had not planned to do so and there was no particular reason that I knew of, but I also knew all reflection on the issue was irrelevant. So up to her house I strode as fast as I could.

I let myself in by the side entrance and called out her name. Annie was in the back room off her study, weeping and alone. Her mother led her own life as much as possible, and that was as everyone wished it to be, particularly Annie. There was no reason for her to "baby-sit" her grown daughter.

"Why Annie!" I rushed to her side. "What ever is the matter?"

"How did you happen to come here, Joe?"

"I don't know, Honey. I just knew I had to come to see you right away."

Annie was dumbstruck. "I was so depressed I didn't know what to do. I needed you terribly."

"The overwhelming thing," I agreed, "is the fact that I didn't know you needed me, but God did. He literally propelled me to your house."

From such a fragile episode as this, a new beginning was launched. Annie and I started meeting regularly for sharing and prayer. The job at the nursery school continued, but gradually we began to realize that she had drives and ambitions which her education had not equipped her to fulfill. She also needed some physical and spiritual space between herself and her parents to finish the process of breaking away from them and the anger-producing dependency she still felt.

So back to school she went, first to Syracuse University, then to the University of Illinois where she became a familiar and loved figure on the campus at Urbana. Four and one-half years later she took her Ph.D. in psychology.

When those hard, long-working years at Illinois were over she persevered again and this time was successful in finding a job away from home. She has subsequently held several positions in facilities for the handicapped. She is now on the staff of a state hospital in Iowa handling clinical problems and doing research. She is financially independent, and for one whose lifelong battle with dependency has been extreme, that is a matter of major importance.

At the second place where she worked, in her persevering search for a permanent companion-helper, she found Natalie. Natalie was a six-and-a-half year resident of the institution, suffering some limitations of the mind. Annie however recognized her potential and asked to have Natalie assigned to her residence. Natalie blossomed under Annie's caring. She had not had a home of her own for many years. Her love and gratitude to Annie was unlimited. She couldn't do enough to please her. She learned to understand Annie's speech quite readily, to cook and clean, to help Annie with life's thousand necessities.

It is now a partnership which goes back over 10 years. Each is profoundly grateful for the other. Natalie's admiration for her "Dr. Annie" is equaled by Annie's admiration for Natalie's phenomenal growth.

Every year when I see Annie, I'm impressed with the continual honing of her professional skills, the improvement of her speech, the depth of her insight, the reality of her maturity. But when I think of the price of each new beginning, the sheer stubborn, trustful shouldering each day of that day's burden, year after year, I can only mumble some kind of inadequate stammer of thanksgiving.

Being involved as I have for almost three decades in the ministry of healing, it was natural that Annie and I should have on numerous occasions asked God to intervene directly in her affliction. Annie had heard and read much about Oral Roberts, and on one summer day long ago she asked me if I would drive her to Trenton where Oral Roberts was having a healing mission.

When we got to Trenton we were given a ticket admitting us to a special tent for people in wheelchairs and on stretchers. Ambulances were arriving with the sick, and the place was nearly full. However I found a spot where I could sit on the ground beside Annie's chair. A loudspeaker carried the service to our tent, and I remember that Roberts was preaching on the three men cast into the fiery furnace. "But there was a fourth one, according to the king, like an angel," Roberts said, "and there is an angel of Christ's healing here with us today."

Presently Roberts came into the tent where we were waiting. Unquestionably a power, a mighty force of some kind entered with him. Roberts moved from bed to chair, touching each person with vigor and claiming in the name of Jesus Christ that they were healed. When he left the tent there was pandemonium. Wailing, weeping, loud praising could be heard from all sides.

I have never doubted that Roberts is a man of spiritual gifts, nor do I question that many have been healed and blessed by his ministry. His style is not mine, nor should it be. On that day long ago in a tent in Trenton, New Jersey, he was a man willing to be foolish for Christ; and many were helped.

But Annie was something else. She was straining to say

something. It was hard to hear in the hubbub. "I want to walk," she said.

Eagerly I folded back the footsteps of the chair and helped her to her feet. Perspiring with the effort, she put one foot in front of the other. Then she grabbed my arm to steady herself as she backed into her chair again. Nothing was different. We were both struck dumb with disappointment.

"Let's go home," she murmured at last.

I pushed her chair over the dusty grass to the parking lot, and we drove home in almost total silence. Annie subsequently experienced one of the deepest depressions she had ever had. In her weariness and confusion there was a temptation to give it all up, but the One who is able to keep us from falling did not fail us.

God always holds out a new beginning, but sometimes His purpose can be thwarted by the wrong match between method and need. The approach doesn't fit the person. The answer is not the one intended for that problem at that time. In our enthusiasm to help, we often rush in with answers which have been effective in previous situations but are not appropriate to the one at hand. We need to take time to find the Lord's launch pad rather than simply assume we know what it is. That was my mistake in taking Annie to Trenton; I never once stopped to ask for the leading of the Lord in the matter. The failure of the effort and the depression which followed were not Oral Roberts' responsibilities; they were ours.

The wisdom of waiting for the right prayer at the right time is something we learned some years afterwards from Agnes Sanford. It was 1953 or 1954 when Agnes consented to come to Swathmore, Pennsylvania, to conduct a healing mission in our church. It was a wonderful time for all of us as we were led into new dimensions of prayer.

At one point, not by any prearranged appointment, Annie

and Agnes met in the front of the church face to face. From her wheelchair Annie looked up at Agnes and asked if she believed the Lord was capable of healing her through Agnes' prayers. Agnes responded with deep compassion that she did not have the faith for such a prayer. She would need time, she added, to discover how God wanted her to pray for Annie. Annie accepted that.

A year or so later Agnes returned to us for another mission. It was a cold, snowy, February night, but in spite of the weather the church was full of people eager to learn more from this great teacher. Annie and her family were in the congregation.

Agnes spoke about the parable of the seed and the sower, drawing analogies between our prayers as the seeds and our lives as the ground. After the service, Annie's father went up to Agnes and asked her if she would come to their pew and pray for his daughter. He didn't know about Annie's previous conversation with Agnes the year before.

It was therefore a surprise to Annie when she saw her father and Mrs. Sanford coming toward the pew where she was sitting. Annie told me that she suddenly became two persons, a participant and an observer. The observer was horrified at Annie's reaction.

"No, no!" she cried out to Agnes. "Don't come!"

At the close of the formal service, I had slipped out of the church and gone to my study. I had no sooner sat down than I felt a compulsion to get up and race back to the sanctuary. As I came into the church I heard the desperation in Annie's voice.

Annie saw me at once and began to sob.

I said, "Annie, dear, don't cry. You can do that later." I glanced at Agnes standing uncertain in the aisle. "Would you two like a chance to talk?"

Both women said yes, and so it was arranged. I told

Annie's parents to go on home; I would bring Annie later in my car. The three of us went to my study together.

Agnes went over to the window and stood looking at the white snowflakes still swirling about the light posts in the parking lot. At last she came to where we were waiting, Annie in her wheelchair, I perched on a corner of the desk.

"You know," Agnes began, "the Lord Jesus could do it, but I can't believe for the healing of cerebral palsy. It would be like asking a tinker toy engine to pull a Pennsylvania railroad train from Philadelphia to New York. I haven't the strength to channel that much power. But I do know what God desires for us tonight. He has given me the power to heal your urge for suicide."

Annie and I looked at each other, startled.

I said, "Just yesterday Annie told me she wanted to die."

Agnes smiled. "There was a time when I could not go near a high window for fear of jumping out." She looked at Annie. "Do you want me to pray for you to be healed of this desire?"

Annie nodded. I knelt by her side while Agnes put her hands on Annie's head. She prayed about the rejection and frustration of Annie's past, and she asked the Lord to heal her desire for self-destruction.

Later Annie told me that as Agnes prayed for her, she felt a warmth flow through her "like a cup of hot, clear soup." There was a glowing radiance in the weeks and months which followed. A new beginning in Christ had come when we found the right match between method and need. It was the right prayer for the right time. Agnes would not leave the window that snowy night until she received the Lord's specific guidance. She knew Jesus was for Annie in some important, immediate way. Then it came to her: the urge to give up trying. That needed healing, and this was the moment for the specific, God-given new beginning.

Who knows? Only God knows whether Annie might still be healed through some tremendous miracle of her physical affliction. In the meantime she has persevered from college to graduate work, to her doctorate, to employment, to research, to professional value and competence, to independence, to service for others, to witnessing for Christ in countless lives across the nation.

It has not been a straight line. It never is. That is where trust comes in. Along with the new beginnings there have been hosts of disappointments. Colleagues have challenged her capacities. Setbacks have occurred. People continue to regard her as a "poor creature." But Annie perseveres, insisting she be treated as a person, struggling and overcoming, like the rest of us.

One of Annie's deepest struggles has always been with loneliness. Her mother is now in her 80s, frail, coping with never-ending pain from shingles—an affliction of the nervous system. Natalie is loyal, good, helpful, but there are worlds of experience which Annie cannot share with her. Throughout Annie's life she has suffered from the desire to be like everyone else, free to come and go, to act and decide as others do. Deeper than all this is her longing to love and be loved as others love. Yet, in all directions, her physical limitations have compelled her to make accommodations with her desires. The result has been repeated plunges into the abyss of loneliness and frustration.

At various crisis times in her professional adult life we have talked long distance on the telephone. "No one understands, Joe. Sometimes I'm so lonely I don't know what to do."

Annie's problem is one that all of us know. The only difference is one of degree. I often say to people as I have to Annie, "Jesus was tested in the desert alone, and so are we. Jesus had to drink the cup of his destiny alone, and so must we. Jesus stood in the judgment hall alone, and we too are judged alone. Jesus had to die alone, and so do we. Each of us must persevere in the pit of loneliness one by one, seeking the hand of the Lord, certain that He is already seeking ours."

It is easy to say that faith should be strong enough to overcome our loneliness, but when clouds form, it is impossible either to feel the sun or to see it. There is nothing left but endurance, as many widows and widowers know. I'm afraid that sometimes no effort we exert can make us feel the light however desperately we long for it. But mark this well. The feeling of forsakenness is no proof of being forsaken. I do not know whether my mother borrowed the phrase or originated it, but in talking to me about my father's death she said, "Remember, mourning after an absent God is an evidence of love as strong as rejoicing in a present one." A person may be more deeply committed to the Lord Jesus while crying out in bewilderment and grief, than when mouthing empty phrases of praise and thanksgiving.

In times of deep loneliness, there is only one thing to do: persevere in trust. The sun is there even if you can't see it or feel it. Or if you cannot trust, if it is one of those awful hours when the windows of the soul are darkened and doubt overwhelms your heart, persevere in hope. When your nerves are shattered and your energies are gone and life is too much for you, then faith must give way to longing. Let the psalmist say it for you: "O my soul . . . hope thou in God: for I shall yet praise Him for the help of His countenance."

I have said it to Annie, to those in the coils of grief, to people suffering the betrayal of love, as in the case of Ken's jealousy and Nancy's alcoholism. Don't try to find consolation in feelings; they are the mercury in all of us. Like the ebb and tide of the sea, they are ever in motion. In a low state of emptiness and loneliness everything takes on the coloration of our own dark greyness. But like the darkness before the dawn, this is precisely the moment when new birth is most likely to occur. In my experience it is not when we are most energetic and optimistic that the deep renewal of our life occurs but at exactly those times when we have reached the end of our own strength, and even faith.

Persevere in hope, and you will wake one morning and know the presence of One in whom there is no variableness, nor shadow, nor turning away; the Lord, who is the same yesterday, today and tomorrow. This is our ground of hope. Find the company of those who can believe, even when you cannot. And I promise you it will happen: the dear Savior will enter your soul and fill you with His love.

Annie often tells me she wouldn't be here now were it not for new beginnings granted her again and again after seasons of emptiness. She belongs to the Lord and He belongs to her. That's the reality, whatever the weather of the moment.

At commencement exercises in 1978, Drew University recognized the rarity of Annie's spirit—her faith, her perseverance, her service to others and her witness to the Lord's love—by voting to confer on her an honorary degree.

After the president of the university telephoned the news to Annie, she called me long distance: "You have been a part of my long haul. I want you there."

As Annie's mother and Natalie, my wife Peggy and I sat in the audience that May afternoon and heard Annie's career described, my heart nearly stopped with pride. Her work with airmen undergoing treatment; with disabled students at the University of Illinois; her research which led to new methods of evaluating the potential of profoundly

retarded people, especially infants; her development of tech
niques never before used for such patients, resulting in a
growth in severely retarded children never before achieved
her published work recognized by the American Psychologi-
cal Association; it all added up to a breath-taking contribution. In the words of the summary: "Her service to other
people, her compassion are products of an ever-deepening
Christian faith." Making the citation, the president said
"Because you enable the rest of us to see what it means
to be truly normal, I confer upon you the degree, Doctor
of Humane Letters."

As I looked at Annie's glowing face that day, all I could
think was, "Thank You, Lord, for hanging in with us as
we hang in with You." A holy intimacy, a victory worth
all the perseverance, sat before me in a wheelchair that
May day, shining out of a pair of bright blue eyes. How
many new beginnings had led to that day? Only she and
I and God knew the answer. Thank God she and the Lord
never gave up.

Chapter 8

Finding Happiness

NATURALLY IN THINKING back over 60 years of friendships, I have chosen to write about those lives whose new beginnings have been most visible because the problems were extreme. Often it takes a magnifying glass to help us see ourselves. However, lest the labor of faith appear to be a grim business, I want to describe the joy—the happiness—which is the essential characteristic of the Christian walk. Happiness is what new beginning is all about.

Jesus told us that He came that our "joy might be full," and each new birth in Him is a birth into some new dimension of this joy. But what is this happiness He promises? Let us see if we can find a definition with which we would all agree.

All of us in the human family seek the pleasures of life. There are the pleasures of comfort and sleep, the pleasures of protection from cold and heat. There are the pleasures of food, taste, and drink. There are the pleasures of tenderness and passion, of sexual playfulness and fulfillment.

There are the pleasures of old and new sights and sounds. There are the pleasures of physical exercise and skill, the pleasures of entertainment in sports and the theatre. There are the pleasures of esthetics: beauty in all its endless forms of dance, music, painting, sculpture, architecture. There are the pleasures of words: poetic words, dramatic words, fictional words, language in all its manifold facets. There is the ceaseless fascination of beauty in the human body, in nature in her boundless moods and seasons, from the stride of Perseus across the night sky to the strange mixture of moonlight and sea tides in the rhythm of a woman's blood.

All of these pleasures are gifts of the Creator to the creature. They belong to all of us, though not equally. Most people appreciate a few of these pleasures intensely, are indifferent to others. Health and economics are obviously related to any individual's range of possible enjoyment. And for millions in our culture, the pursuit of pleasure is the limit of their vision of happiness. Their energy, their thirst for money and power are motivated by their drive to experience life's pleasures. I do not wish to make judgments about such people. I have loved many such folk, and not a few of them are among the most delightful and interesting people I have ever known.

In the summer of 1939, in Paris, I met an Italian family who had long lived in France. A member of that family, Guido, befriended me as an equal, though he was 20 years older. He taught me more about beauty than I have ever learned from books.

He loved all the arts, especially theatre and the opera. He was a small-boned, dark, thin, intense, passionate person whose every reaction was expressed as though he were Adam newly set down in the garden. No one before him had ever heard *Aida;* Verdi had composed it just for Guido.

The famous Van Gogh *Haystack* was alive with the flaming warmth of summer only in Guido's eyes.

His immediacy before all beauty belonged to his nature. He could not help himself. I have seen him stop stock-still before a truly beautiful woman on the street, staring with sincerest awe. Once we encountered a street performer who played a mouth organ held in his teeth, beat a drum with one foot, wore a hat to which there were attached several rows of tingling bells, played the violin with his hands, and operated a rig which made a triangle strike at appropriate moments with his other foot. Guido was spellbound. "Look at that, Joseph; it's a miracle!" He walked over to where the musician's violin case lay open on the curb and in a dramatic gesture turned his pockets inside out to show that every coin they possessed had been given to this wonder.

There were several women in his life, though never two at the same moment. Each one was the idol of his heart. There had never been such a love before! He was insanely jealous. Every woman he loved had to be his sole possession. She had to rise with the intensity of his enthusiasms and fall with the depth of his depressions. His passion was all-consuming for a season, and then suddenly he would become indifferent for reasons no one could ever fathom— Guido least of all, I suspect.

I never saw a trace of malice or cruelty in Guido. Even in his love life, when sudden shifts in the winds of passion changed everything between himself and his current attachment, he was gnawed by guilt, abject in his apologies, tearful in his confessions, accusing himself of the most depraved nature God had ever conceived.

I went with him one time into Notre Dame. We sat down near a large bank of prayer candles. Old women shuffled in to light tapers, cross themselves and bend heavily to their knees. Young women with shining eyes gazed on the too-brightly-painted figure of the blessed Virgin before they also left a flickering taper behind. An occasional young man would appear, tentative, almost furtive. For some reason I turned my head to look at Guido. To my great surprise I saw that he was weeping, making no effort to stanch the flow of tears. He merely sat there and watched the faithful come and kneel and walk away in peace.

Presently a great organ, the king of instruments, began to sing under the expert fingers of an obviously accomplished organist. Guido got up quickly and motioned for me to follow him. He went directly to a door I could barely see. Together we inched our way up the winding staircase until we came to the organ loft.

Apparently the organist knew him. He nodded a greeting at us and continued without interruption to play this incomparable instrument. We sat in the shadows of the console, entranced by the genius of this great musician, with not a sheet of music before him, improvising on a theme with endless imagination and power. Up in that loft the volume of sound was enormous; I became the music. It filled me totally.

After awhile we crept down as we had come up. At the bottom of the stairs Guido turned to me and whispered, "Joseph, always place yourself in life where you can tremble before beauty."

And yet with all his immense sensitivity to the beautiful, his enormous capacity for pleasure, Guido was not a happy man. The pleasures he enjoyed in such rich measure served to bind him to a continual pursuit of newer, stronger sensations. I occasionally sensed in him a wistfulness for something deeper, but as long as I knew him it was never more than a poignant longing.

True happiness is more than pleasure. It is also freedom.

There is a craving in the human heart best described as a thirst for the infinite. We seem to be so made that nothing which has limits satisfies. I have often pondered the question: What is the deepest urge in the human breast? What is it that we would willingly die for? Is it love? Perhaps. Is it justice? Sometimes. Or is it freedom? In the scale of values, I must confess I come out again and again on the side of freedom. Without it, justice so easily becomes tyranny; love so easily becomes malignant possessiveness.

Do you know that feeling I prize in the presence of boundlessness? Don't you often have a sense of expansion and peace come over you when you take a solitary walk along the ocean or sail out upon its surface, beyond the sight of another creature or craft? Isn't it the same when you stand at the top of a Swiss alp or walk in a forest on a still, dark night? There is a mirror in the soul to all that is infinite. Something innate within us rejoices in all that is vast, unlimited, unfettered, free.

In his memoirs the Greek writer Nikos Kazantzakis tells of the occasion when Crete became free after a long and cruel struggle. His father took him by the hand and led him out of their village to the local cemetery. He scraped away some soil on Nikos' grandfather's grave. Into this depression he saw his father insert his mouth as deeply as he could. Three times he cried out, "Father, we are free. We are free. We are free!"

I've often wondered what it means to read in Genesis that God made us in His image. Surely a part of the meaning must be that some faint fragment of the divine infinitude was poured into the strange chemistry of our being. Infinity is a part of us. Never to rest is the price we pay for being human. Infinite goodness, boundless peace, a beauty which eye has never yet seen, a justice which has no shadow of corruption, a righteousness which has no blemish of self-satisfaction: "As the hart panteth after the water brooks so panteth my soul after Thee, O God."

Lady Poverty set Francis free to live out the boundless love of Christ until he broke even the boundaries of time haunting generations of Christians with his incomparable witness. The patient grace of God freed Augustine from the tyranny of flesh and pride to be reborn in the power of Christ and become a saint of Christendom whose words will be read until the final trumpet is sounded and the Lord of Glory comes again.

True joy is ours in all those sacred moments when we break out of our bondages to pleasure, power, wealth—all our petty prison-houses of sin. It comes each time we affirm our freedom as creatures of infinitude and children of eternity.

But there is still more. Happiness is love. We are happiest not just in the midst of enjoyments or when we are freed from the web of private sins and collective tragedy, but when we are in the presence of someone we love. Are there any moments in life quite like those moments when we are truly present, open, available to someone we love, and that person is available to us? To accept and to be accepted as you are, for the person you are, exactly as you are, with all your ambiguities and inconsistencies and contradictions, "warts and all"; to be loved because you are, not for what you say or do or have; surely this must be the quality of happiness the blessed Lord desires for all of us.

I must confess I never knew that special, unconditional kind of love on a human plane until Peggy came into my life. She is a lovely woman with her green eyes, brown hair and trim figure. With her radiant smile she looks much younger than her years. I sometimes tell people she is 20 years younger than I am, and they often believe it.

The great thing she has taught me is a quality of loving

I had only known from afar before she brought this happiness to my life. When I tell her how overcome I am by her caring for me, not as I'd like to be or as I sometimes fool myself that I am, but just *as* I am, she says, "It's easy." But I'm not all that easy to bear. She is a very private and reserved person to everyone but me, and it fills me with wonder that she should choose to give herself to me so unreservedly.

The Savior couldn't possibly have demonstrated how everlastingly He is for me, nor how truly *new beginning* is another term for *happiness,* in any more convincing way than to have given me Peggy in marriage at this late hour. She tells me she feels the same way. For her it is due to the Lord's providence and that's the end of the question.

She is a direct and spontaneous person, her faith more childlike and trustful than mine. When she was a girl she made her commitment to Christ, and it has remained the core of her being, free of complexity or anguish. Her rebirth in the Spirit, like mine, has been a continuing experience, with peak times which belong to her own privacy. But I have shared some of them in the last couple of years and I know the waters of her soul are deep. Happiness is love.

And even yet we have not touched bottom. Happiness is peace. St. Paul writes, "And let the peace of God rule in your hearts." Jesus invites us to rest in his peace: "Come unto me all ye that labour and are heavy laden, and I will give you rest." Even the world of nature responds to his command, "Peace, be still"; and the storm abates. Before his earthly departure He says, "Peace I leave with you, my peace I give to you." The Gospel story begins and ends with peace. At the nativity the angels sing of peace to all the earth, and at His resurrection the Savior pronounces His characteristic benediction upon His frightened disciples: "Peace. It is I."

Here is a depth of happiness which is greater than pleasure by far, deeper even than freedom or love. Freedom and love have to be compromised in the harsh realities of existence. Accommodations have constantly to be made between what we expect from ourselves and one another and what we achieve. In our first year of marriage I filled Peggy with not a little dismay because I was expecting her to be someone she was not. There are always tensions between our expectations and our performance, even in our loving. The world about us brims over with the contradictions between our professions of justice and the realities of our social existence. But the peace of God is to be experienced not in the absence of these discordances but in their very midst. We stop trying to do it by ourselves. We remember that the Lord is for us just as we are. In the midst of our imperfection and brokenness we rest in His peace.

All else in creation is becoming. Only God is, as He revealed to Moses on Mount Sinai when He announced His name, "I am." There is no discord between God's love and His power, between His justice and His being, between His truth and His word. An infinite peace arises out of the divine harmony of His presence.

There is the peace of Lago Maggiore spread before my feet. There is the peace of the Alps around me wearing their crown of snow, now luminous in the setting sun. There is the peace of a long labor well done and finished. There is the peace of death. But none of this is the peace which Christ promises us. His is the living peace of His indescribable love for us, not only for the world and all people, but for you and for me. Never forget that the signature of the Holy Spirit most universally recognized is peace.

Now at last we come to the bottom of what happiness is. It is the knowledge of being in Christ. St. John and St. Paul make it the center of all they have to tell us. Matthew, Mark, and Luke proclaim the Gospel and we are reverently grateful for every word, but St. John and St. Paul show us what it is to be in the heart of the One whose Gospel they live to affirm. St. Paul never wearies of rejoicing that "whether we live . . . or die . . . we are the Lord's." Christ in us! That is St. Paul's victory cry. And in a different key it is also St. John's song. In that incomparable, sacred prayer recorded in the 17th chapter of John's Gospel, Jesus prays that He may be in us, "I in them, and Thou in Me, that they may be made perfect . . ."

Is this not the flame of Christly joy? We are in Him as He is in us! We are as greatly loved as God loved His only begotten Son. There is no other happiness, no other joy worthy of the name.

When Christ is in us and we are in Him, we have found the pearl, the treasure in the field which is worth everything and anything to possess. It is the pearl of His consummate love from which we can never be separated. It is the light which illumines and sanctifies all the other dimensions of happiness. It is the power which renews and regenerates all our experiences of pleasure, freedom and love.

The vision of St. John on the island of Patmos, with which the Bible ends, is full of joy. It is a tapestry of unspeakable plentitude: golden crowns, precious stones, resplendent robes, shining seas, a thousand-voiced choir. The vision closes with the holy assurance of happiness without end: "And God shall wipe away all tears from their eyes; and there shall be no more . . . crying, neither . . . any more pain." This is the ultimate, the eternal beginning, to which all our beginnings here on earth are tending.

Now I wish you would quietly compose your spirit, and if possible and desirable, ask someone you cherish to read these words to you as though the living Christ were lovingly speaking them aloud while you listen with closed eyes. If you are alone, shift your posture, breathe deeply and read these words slowly to yourself. Imagine the Master saying:

"What happiness it is to complete My joy by being with you. It is well that we are together. Your face is beautiful to Me. I know your every expression. I know well that hooded, withdrawn look when you separate yourself from Me. And when you look into My eyes and I see a rekindling of the warm fire that burns in you for Me and for those you love, I rejoice that you know that nothing can separate us. I sing when your eye leaps to meet the flame of a cardinal winging his redness through the summer green. I smile when I watch you take a deep breath and complete the task I have given you. It gladdens me when I see your reverence for everyone you know as well as for My freedom to deal with each one as the wind of My Spirit prompts. Your humility in the presence of My creation, the honor you give to the universe which the Father and I have made, your openness to My truth everywhere, your incessant reach for purity and excellence, your obedience to My word makes you precious beyond all price to Me. When you forget yourself by giving yourself to My kingdom among the poor, the oppressed, the misused, the blind and indifferent, the lost and the angry—you move Me to tears of gratitude. It is well we are together. My joy in you is great.

"Are you asking Me about your sins? Do I hear you pleading with Me about your times of betrayal? Are you whispering to Me about your disloyalties, your double-minded conflicts? Do not flee from Me. When you fail yourself, you do not fail Me. Your deceptions and 'twistyness,' your meanness and pettiness are all opportunities for Me. I rise in eager expectation as you face your own truth. 'Now,' I say to Myself, 'there will be a turning to Me. A new beginning is now possible. A renewal of trust in My love is about to take place.' And when it doesn't happen, I wait with undiminished hope for the next opportunity.

"Don't you realize there is nothing you can do to change My love for you? I see the shadows as well as the light. I have watched you walk into a wilderness of inner destructiveness, becoming more and more closed in upon yourself, troubled and unloving, piling guilt on top of guilt, rebellion on top of rebellion. You thought you had driven even Me from your life. Don't you know you can't stop Me from loving you? How My heart aches for you.

"Will you hear me now? Listen! I have gone with you into your private world of destruction, and I love you more than ever. My love abides. You are always more to Me than what you do or what you say or how you appear. To Me you are always you. The self I love and will always love is not yours to dispose of as you wish. A love which ceases to be is not My love. You belong to Me, as you belong to no one else, and I will never let you go. I am in you that your joy may be full."

Chapter 9

Endings and Beginnings

WE CANNOT CONCLUDE this book on new beginnings without seeing God's love at the end of life. For as T. S. Eliot has said, "In our ending is our beginning." Jesus is indeed for us most vividly at the end.

Among many other things, the sainted Pope John XXIII showed Christians how to die. In spite of much pain he refused to be over-medicated. It was important to him to be as aware as possible of what was happening at the close of his life. Why? The clue is the crucifix which was on the wall at the foot of his bed. He insisted that no one be permitted to obscure his view of the dying Christ. His eyes seldom left that suffering figure at the end of his bed. In a depth we cannot fathom, Pope John and the Lord Jesus were one in those final hours. This was the joy he did not want to miss, however well-intended the ministrations of his doctors may have been. He knew the Lord would be with him to the last and he wanted also to be with the Lord.

Since in a parish the size of ours, deaths occur at least 30 times a year, naturally by now I have seen hundreds of people die. Each death is different from every other one. But one characteristic has struck me with breath-taking intensity. It is the unmistakable sense of labor so often observable at the end among those who are aware that their hour has come. It can only be likened to the labor pains of birth. Something awesome and of the greatest gravity is taking place. The essential person before me is laboring to enter an altogether different dimension. Not infrequently it is a torturous business. The body doesn't want to let go; the soul must struggle to get free. The person succeeds briefly in loosening the harsh grip of the flesh, and victory is in sight. A few minutes later the grip has tightened again, and the person once more wrestles with the flesh of his outworn dwelling place. So it goes until finally, "the strife is o'er, the battle won." It is these experiences which have convinced me that death and birth are not opposites but analogies.

Today is Sunday. I went to the 6:30 A.M. mass at St. Martin's. I was awakened by the bells of the nearby tower; their claim on me was irresistible and I dressed quickly. There were about 100 of us, perhaps more. I watched the faces of these exuberant people, many of them browned and lined from long hours spent on mountain terraces mending and pruning the vineyards. As they went up to receive the sacrament from the hands of the priest, they emanated a reverence that touched my very bones. This was holy food indeed! And when they came back to their seats it was not the boredom of long familiarity I saw on their faces but radiant joy. "Christ is risen!" I wanted to say since we are still in the afterglow of Easter. I'm sure that if I had said it in comprehensible Italian, they would have responded, "Christ is risen indeed!"

Perhaps there were some skeptics in St. Martin's at the early mass this morning. But I doubted it, as I walked out with them and stood about the courtyard commenting in feeble Italian on the beauty of the lake shrouded in the early fog, soon to be dispersed by the brightness we could see above the eastern peaks. What a privilege is theirs, living out their lives in such a setting! To them it would be the most gross scandal to be told they are not essentially souls. They know they are persons who will, at death, move into the Father's many-mansioned kingdom. It is evident in the dignity with which they quietly carry themselves.

I know Scripture predicts an end time when the Lord of judgment will bring a close to the human story, and the souls of the righteous will rise, and I often wonder if the Judgment Day is not palpably near. Yet I also believe Jesus meant it literally when He said to the penitent thief, "*This day* you will be with me in paradise." Both things can be true. They do not preclude one another. What is important is that both attest to the immortality of the soul. "The souls of the just are in the hand of God," the third chapter of the Book of Wisdom tells us:

> And no torment shall reach them.
> They seemed in view of the foolish, to be dead
> And their passing away was judged an affliction
> And their going forth from us, utter destruction.
> But they are in peace.
> For if before men indeed they be perished
> Yet is their hope full of immortality.
> Chastised a little, they shall be greatly blessed
> Because God tried them and found them worthy of himself.
> As gold in the furnace, he proved them,
> And as sacrificial offerings he took them to himself.

John Donne touched this dimension of our faith with extraordinary depth and beauty:

They shall awake as Jacob did and say as Jacob said
Surely the Lord is in this place
And this is no other than the house of God and the gate of
  heaven.
And into that gate they shall enter and in that house they
  shall dwell
Where there shall be no cloud nor sun
No darkness nor dazzling but one equal light
No noyse nor silence but one equal musik
No fears nor hopes but one equal possession
No foes or friends but one equal communion and identity,
Nor ends, nor beginnings, but one equal eternity.

The resurrection is the hinge of the One who said He was the door into a new life. This man of Nazareth was not simply a genius of the spirit in whose presence there was an emanation of power and healing, nor was He merely a gifted prophetic figure reforming and chastening the legalism of Judaism. He was the Son of God, unique, irreplaceable, speaking the word of everlasting truth. Do we accept the authority of this One whom we call Lord? Do we believe the word of this One in whom the message and the messenger are one? If we do, then we are content to rest in His assurance that "where I am, there ye may be also," and to accept His resurrection as the seal of His promise that death is only a new beginning.

And if we do not . . .

It grieves my heart to remember how often I have seen the absence of this faith among the dying. Millicent Graham comes to my mind at once. She was a physician married to a physician. Her short-cropped, grey hair, the long face with its strong chin and horned-rimmed glasses loom before me now. She always wore flat, square heels and tweed suits. What a rare, deep person she was! In my study closet I have pages and pages of the poetry she wrote in medical school. There's not a single one which is not in the minor key of hope deferred, love unfulfilled, faith unfound; yet they are resplendent with superb images of flowers, woods, furry creatures, birds, light and darkness.

Millicent was somehow a bird in a cage. Even when the door opened for her, some fear or despair prevented her from taking flight. Life only confirmed her worst intimations of a tragic future. Her college-age eldest son committed suicide. She and I together cut the rope from which he was dangling grotesquely in the attic. I'll never blot from my mind the memory of Millicent holding her boy's body in her lap and moaning like David of the Bible, "Oh Robert, my son, Robert."

Her marriage was impossible. She had done everything any rational person could do to save it. Her husband was a good man, but he never understood her, and I suspect she never understood him. I can see him now, dark hair unkempt, clothes rumpled, tie askew, striding alone to Robert's grave, head held high, irrationally refusing to believe it had been a suicide.

A few years after Robert's death they parted. She took a position as the physician of a prestigious women's college in the East. She was never one to have many friends, but she always cultivated a few choice ones, and at her home there was soon a small circle who saw the rarity of the person among them: gracious, intellectually keen, sensitive, humorous, artistic. I believe these were her happiest years, save those when her three boys were small.

Then cancer of the stomach overcame her. I made several trips to visit her, seeing her for the last time only days before her death, then returning to conduct her memorial service in the college chapel.

On our last visit I pulled a chair close to her bed in the college infirmary. She was half reclining, holding my hand. Toward the end we prayed together. She confessed how hard it was for her to believe and trust. I told her that sometimes we had to accept another's faith when we found it impossible to stand on our own, and for both of us I claimed a new beginning in the Savior's love.

I would have given anything for Millicent to have flown from her cage that evening when I opened the door, to have accepted the new life the Savior held out to her, but I'm sure she died with a question still on her lips.

These things are too much for me. I know what the love in me tells me, and I am careful not to judge lest I be judged, as Jesus admonishes. It is all in His care, and there I leave it, albeit with a sad and heavy heart. I'm sure the Lord was for Millicent at a hundred different turning points in her life, but my dear friend could not believe it or trust it, however often I pled for it, analyzed it, prayed about it.

How different is the experience of those whose faith is radiantly present at the end. Many such ones come to my memory now. Jim Satterfield was a man in his late 40s. He was southern, courteous, thoughtful of others, a business executive, smooth-faced, brown-eyed. He was married to a vivacious blonde named Candy. Both of them had important experiences of rebirth in the Lord in England while Jim was working for his company's operations there. I couldn't believe my ears when Jim told me he was going into Memorial Hospital for treatment of a brain tumor. The malignancy turned out to be beyond control.

Jim's faith was something no one who knew him will ever forget. It was common knowledge that he was dying. Jim never tried to deny it to himself nor to others. He was frank to say that he would like to win the struggle for health and that it grieved him deeply to leave his family. Yet as his end grew near, he accepted it with the same grace which was the hallmark of his character.

When people asked him about his equanimity he would say, "It's nothing remarkable—I'm in the Lord's hands. Whether I live or whether I die, I am His."

"I wish I could have your faith, Jim," people would say.

"You can!" he would answer with emphasis. "Trust Him."

When he died, Candy told me there was a wondrous peace on his face. Everyone who visited him at the last noticed it. He gave peace to others because he had it himself. He knew the Lord was for him.

I have often said that people die the way they live. Jim died in faith, as he had lived in grace, concerned and considerate of everyone about him.

If anger on the other hand is the predominant response of our lives toward those things we cannot control, we shall die as angry people, unless before the end we find the Lord who is for us. If jealous possessiveness is the characteristic way in which we have related to the anxieties of life, we shall die as bitter people, unless we find the Lord who is for us. If fear has been the dominant response of our lives to each day's events, then we will die in terror, unless we find the Lord who is for us. If cynicism has been our attitude toward the deepest questions of life, then we will die as empty stoics determined perhaps only to spare the feelings of others, unless we find the Lord who is for us. If the shadow of guilt has been like a pall on all that is beautiful and good in our life, then we will die with a dreadful sense of remorse, unless we find the Lord who is for us.

When, however, we do find the joy of the Lord's presence, even if the discovery is like a shooting star illumining our sky but for a moment, then we shall die with peace on our faces, ready to accept this final new beginning, ready to see what is in the garden on the other side of the wall.

It is the inevitable question: Shall we live and meet again? Far below my balcony here in Switzerland I can see a small portion of a narrow, winding road at the foot of the mountain, weaving its tortuous way around the contours of this land which drops in perpendicular lines to the edge of the lake. It is a road which was built by the Romans before the Christian era. Death is like that Roman road. It is life's most ancient and important question, but like the road below me, I can only see that which belongs to my present vision. I cannot see around the mountain bend, but I trust that when I get there, the Master will be waiting to show me the way.

That is how it was with Pat. No funeral I have ever conducted was as difficult for me as the one in which I buried her three small daughters who had died in the fire which consumed her house.

"Faulty wiring," the fire chief told us.

All I remember of that awful, dark night was holding the hands of Bob and Pat and weeping with them in the home of Bob's parents. What is comfort? It is not to speak words, however pious and true. It is to weep with those who weep, to agonize with those who agonize, to rebel with those who rebel and to wait for the tempest to pass. It is to love without trying to teach or to change anything; just to love and touch hands in the dark.

A few years later Pat's handsome husband, Bob, died in an airplane crash. The knife of separation had fallen again, and the pain was dreadful. But Pat's blue eyes were not as glazed with grief this time as they had been following the deaths of her daughters. Two weeks before Bob died, something had happened to make a difference.

Pat told me she had been awakened in the night. Their bedroom was aglow with a luminous presence. It was a vision of the Lord Jesus. She didn't know what to make of it except to stare at it in amazement and wonder. From that presence there flowed into her a peace and love she had never imagined. She was transfixed with adoration. Then it was gone.

She awakened Bob and told him with awed voice what she had seen. He didn't dismiss it nor scorn it. He merely accepted it as a mysterious thing which had happened.

After Bob's death and in the struggles which followed as she raised the new family she and Bob had started, Pat's faith never wavered. She firmly believes that the vision of the Lord was given to her to sustain her for what was to come, and I believe it too. Along with the unnameable losses she suffered came the unnameable love of Jesus. Pat knows that no matter what, He is for her and for all those whom she loves.

Oh, if we were all more trusting! If we would trust His shepherding care every step of life's journey! The older I get, the more deeply I cherish a quality I detect in little children, for I now know that the deepest secrets are given from the pockets of God only to those whose souls have become childlike.

Yesterday morning as I walked to the village on an errand, there were children playing in the courtyard of a nearby "ristorante." There is a simplicity about these small, merry-eyed creatures whose homes are perched on terraces blasted out of the sides of this mountain.

I have seen them fold their hands and file solemnly into St. Martin's Church as the bells ring. I have seen them dancing improvised jigs which made their friends collapse with hilarious laughter. I have seen them, with wide, round eyes, watch a man play a tuba, then flee in shouting glee as the tuba-man quick-stepped toward them and increased the volume of his wonderful instrument. I have seen them climb the hill behind their village and with the simplest equipment and the flimsiest cloth, sail a kite into the dazzling blue. I have seen them in a downpour of rain transform the village piazza into an oceanfront, using a stick and a wee rag to fabricate a sailing vessel, endlessly happy in damming the water, improvising new harbors, turning unexpected rivulets into mighty rivers. I have seen them at carnival time hop and skip and strut behind their grotesque masks and costumes and felt my heart skip a beat when their mothers pretended not to know them, wondering in wild voices, "Where could little Mario have disappeared to?"

Such children have an abounding capacity for joy. Peguy has a poem in which he says that there is nothing so beautiful in the sight of God as a little child saying, "Our Father," and falling asleep halfway through his first "Hail Mary."

Oh, how I wish I could become childlike. How I wish we could all walk the face of this earth as little children filled with unfading wonder at the beauty of God's handiwork. How I wish my love were more simple, able to rejoice in every day's new gifts. Near our home in Rhode Island is a morning-glory vine. Its blue faces open each day to the sunrise. The sight carries me back in my imagination to the day when I looked at a morning-glory at the age of seven or eight and saw the glory of God. It was a moment of utter thralldom for me. God tries constantly to catch our attention in places and times when His power and majesty and mercy shine through the humble things of this world. When we were little children it happened all the time.

Before I reach the end I earnestly pray that the Lord Christ may have humbled me and refined me sufficiently in the fire of His truth that I shall be ready to enter the kingdom of heaven as a little child. In the meantime, in every agony and crisis of life, it is enough to know that He is for us, offering us His forgiveness, filling us with His joy, freeing us to find new beginnings again—and yet again.